STEEL TOE
REVIEW
VOLUME FOUR

Published by
Tritone Media
5751 9th Avenue South
Birmingham, AL 35212

Cover design by Kevin Van Hyning
Illustrations by Stephen Smith and Nolen Otts
Layout by M. David Hornbuckle

Please visit our website: www.steeltoereview.com

Steel Toe Review: Volume 4
ISBN 978-0-9849495-3-3

Printed in the USA
First printing March 2013
e d c b a

STEEL TOE

REVIEW

VOLUME FOUR

Compiled by the Editors of Steel Toe Review

Tri Tone Media

New York ◆ Birmingham

Table of Contents

Fiction

Visual Art

Editor's Note
M. David Hornbuckle

Welcome to the fourth print issue of Steel Toe Review. It is dedicated to the year 2016, which took away so much of what we admired in the world. Among those heroes and friends who left us in the past year was Nolen Otts. I was first introduced to Nolen by mutual friends twenty-something years ago. He remained on the periphary of my life until his comic strip *Collateral Kids* became a regular feature in *The Birmingham Free Press*, a small newspaper that I edited off and on from 2010-2014. He was a founding member of the Birmingham-based illustrators group, the Cartoonistas. I last saw him in person the day that I asked him to contribute some illustrations to accompany the works that lie within these pages.

This book has been two years in the making because other priorities prevented us from printing a volume in 2015, and this edition is coming out several months later than we initially anticipated. New jobs, late editions, and inconvenient deadlines for other projects made all this take a good bit longer than we planned for it to. Despite the challenges that have faced us in compiling Steel Toe Review #4, it is now here, and we think it looks pretty good.

The work you will find in this volume all has some connection to the American South, although there are times when that connection is rather esoteric. Throughout our history, the most important factor to us is the quality of the writing. The Southern ties may be through theme, characters, settings, or simply through the author's life experience, which may or may not come through in the writing itself. It is all work of considerable quality.

I'd like to thank my staff: Matt Layne, Halley Cotton, Cheyenne Taylor, Jason Walker, Callie Mauldin, and Michael Tesney for helping select material. Thanks also to Kevin Van Hyning for taking on the job of illustrating and designing our cover. Stephen Smith and Nolen Otts did an amazing job of creating original illustrations to accompany some of the stories and poems. Finally, we must thank all the contributors who donated to our Go Fund Me campaign: Brent Stauffer, Robert Eastwood, John Wendel, Lori Lassiter Hamilton, John Saad, Patricia Masterson, Danny Siegel, Adam Vines, Jim Braziel, Billy Palmer, Cathy Rose, Shelly Cato, Foster Dickson, Cameron Enfinger, Ian Hoppe, Liz Hughey, Sarah Houder, George Mostoller, Marc Harshman, Diane Thomas-Plunk, David Langlinais, Dustin Thompson, Jon

Hornbuckle, Angela DiPaolo, Suzanne Rhodenbaugh, Tobi Alfier, Daniel Moore, Ron Pullins, Adam Guthrie, Maria Bittenger, Rob Hunter, Karen Green, Barabara Nishimoto, and William Trent Pancoast.

- M. David Hornbuckle

Suicide at Owl Creek Farm

Dan Jacoby

valley just outside aspen
put a pistol to his head
was frightfully drunk, on drugs
incited mayhem like
huffing ether outside vegas
gonzo journalist
experiencing the truth
manic life force
cavorting with surreal actors

liked his guns
threatened to shoot everyone
marched through doors in woody creek
shotgun leveled at bartender
shooting blanks
setting off smoke bombs
clearing the place
liked his tequila
drank everything
but never wine
couldn't get cork out of bottle

creeks there run hard
laden with trout in spring
as new colts get their legs
drugs and booze
part of the american dream
pushing people's buttons
used a cannon over owl creek
to spread his ashes
fishing was good that spring

Things You Should Know About Me
Wendy Thornton

Jessica leaves the bar at midnight, proud of herself for not closing the place down. She's so drunk she can barely walk. Knows to put one face, no wait, one foot, in front of the other, pace, pace, pace. Keep that rhythm going. Home home home. Don't look up. Don't listen to the guys hollering out their car windows as they drive by. *Hey baby. Wanna fuck? Naw. You're not my type. What's your type? The type that doesn't yell out car windows. Whoooo, man, she burned you. Fuck you, bitch.* The usual. Pace, pace pace.

The neon lights are blinding. She can't remember what else she did besides drink. Someone handed her something. Pills. *You'll like this. What do I have to do for it? Naw, baby, nothing, just try it. There's more where that came from. I'll bet.* She's got no money, so hooking her on something doesn't make good business sense. She ain't coming back for another taste.

Used to be somebody. She could still remember when she was in college, when she had plans. She was going to be a teacher. What a laugh. Imagine, her teaching little kids. *Pay no attention to Ms. Jessica, she's just having a little inner ear problem today.*

She passes the restaurant near her home, a brightly lit Denny's attached to the Holiday Inn. She's happy to know she's so close to home. She's going to make it. One night, she woke up in the parking lot of this very Denny's, her dress over her head. She can't remember what happened. She was sticky down there and sore, so she's pretty sure she got raped. *Report it to the police*, her friend Carol said, and she laughed. *Report what? I woke up with my dress over my head and I'm not sure how it got that way?*

Staggering through the parking lot she looks around warily. It's not the dark spaces you have to worry about. You know they're dangerous. It's the well-lit family places that can catch you, the cheerful smile, the clean-shaven memory of youth. She stares into the windows, finds herself falling towards them, catches herself just as her nose touches the glass.

And there he is, darker than she remembers, his eyes darker. He is talking excitedly to a group of clean cut young men, waving his hands, gesticulating to make a point, laughing as the others respond to whatever he said. He looks over at the windows. His eyes meet hers. He looks startled. He turns back to his buddies. She starts to walk away. A dream. An apparition. Pace, pace, pace.

"Jessica?"

She doesn't want to acknowledge the sound of his voice. She keeps walking. A hand is placed on her shoulder. She wants to slap it off. *Fuck you, you don't know anything about my life. Go back to your bright restaurant and your clean-cut friends.* "It is you, isn't it?" he says.

No plausible deniability. "Hello, Daniel," she tries to purr. She hopes her voice is soft, smooth, but fears that her words are slurred – her mouth is so dry.

He shakes her hand as if it were a dead animal. "It's so good to see you. I was wondering if I'd see any of the old gang this weekend."

"You're just here for the weekend?" Somewhere there's a sinking feeling but she's trying to ignore it. Emotion so far away like a bug buzzing her ear.

"Yeah, just visiting. Had to pick up a certified copy of my degree."

"That would be - ?

"Doctorate."

"Of course."

"How about you, still going to school?"

Fucker, do I look like I'm going to school? My clothes are slutty, my hair smells like vomit and I can't open my eyes all the way. Come to think of it, I do look like a student. "Yeah," she says. "Still going."

He laughs. "Well that's great," he says. "You always did do things your own way." He hesitates, looks towards his friends. "Listen, are you in a hurry? Maybe we could talk?"

His hesitancy pleases her. He was always so sure of himself. When he finished college and went away, he never even asked if she wanted to go with him. For five years they had dated while he worked on his Ph.D. Then suddenly he was finished and just as suddenly he left her behind. She'd have to ask him about that. *What was I,* she would say, *a college interlude? For half a fucking decade?* She'd get revenge. She'd make him want her like he'd never wanted anything.

"Sure," she says leaning towards him seductively, "let's talk."

He gently pushed her backwards. "Let me pick up my check and I'll be right out," he says and disappears into the restaurant. She leans against the wall. The dirty ground spins at her feet. *Whew, gonna be hard to be seductive if I'm throwing up.* She thinks about putting a finger down her throat, getting it over with. But no, maybe it would be more fun to throw up on him.

He comes out of the restaurant, whistling. "My room is on the third

floor," he says, leading her into the hotel lobby. "Just let me just check my messages."

"Waiting for a girlfriend to call?"

He laughs again. His laugh is pleasant, innocent. "No, no girlfriend," he says, leading her to the front desk. "I have a friend overseas who sometimes calls late."

Friend. I'll bet. She looks down at her shoes, scuffed and worn. Her toenails are dirty. Beside her, his feet, in brown sandals, are clean, white, shining in the fluorescent light of the hotel lobby. She is embarrassed by the contrast, her torn sandals, her dirty feet. He wears spotless khaki pants. She wears shredded jeans. He wears a bright yellow polo shirt with some kind of spiffy emblem on the pocket. She wears a halter top that keeps threatening to expose her boobs. He is brilliant. She is blitzed. Always embarrassed from the bottom up. Top down. He was always smarter than she. Not many people were. Of course, that was many brain cells ago. Many lost cells, floating in the ether. *Tell me that you love me,* she thinks. *Take me away and I'll clean up my act.* Even she doesn't believe this, but maybe she'll tell him anyway.

The clerk at the front counter scans her like she's some kind of prostitute. Fucker. How dare he? What does he know about her? When Daniel is finished checking his messages, he leads her to a nearby elevator. As the doors close, she sticks out her tongue at the clerk, whose face remains professionally impassive.

The hotel room is narrow, bland. Off white walls, impressionistic paintings that look mass produced, swirly bedspreads to match. Even the furniture is bland, pale wood that matches the headboards on the double beds. Jessica throws herself down on the nearest bed, her legs open. Daniel doesn't seem to notice. He seats himself gingerly on the edge of the second bed and beams at her.

"I'm so excited to see you again, Jessica. I always hoped I'd run into you again, though I have to admit, I thought the chances were slim you'd still be here."

"Why do you say that?"

"Well, I mean – it's been a while since I left. I thought – "

"You thought I'd finish and be working somewhere?"

"You are so brilliant."

"Ha, that's me. The whiz kid."

"Are you still studying special ed?"

"Not exactly."

"Well, tell me about your life. I want to hear all about it."

She clasps her hands and says with mock enthusiasm, "Do you? Do you really? I'll tell you. There are some things you should know about me. But wait, no, tell me about your life first."

"Mine is pretty dull."

"Do tell, honey."

"Are you okay?"

"I had a few drinks this evening, if that's what you're asking. So, tell me about your life. Where do you work? Making millions?

"Not exactly. I work for a peace organization."

"A what?"

"You've heard of the Dalai Lama?"

"You work for the Dalai Lama?"

"Well, no. I work for a senior minister in Tibet, the Kalon Tripa."

Jessica hooted. "Oooh, trippy."

"I guess you could say that. Right now we're trying to help people affected by the recent earthquake." She looked blank. "You know, in Jiegu?"

Jessica didn't know. "I don't really keep up with current events."

"Oh, well, it doesn't matter. We're trying to raise funds to get people back into some kind of shelter. That's why I'm visiting."

"You always were a real people person," Jessica coos, pulling her knees up to her chest and wrapping her arms around them. She rolls over on her stomach, hunches up into a fetal position. She tries to rise off the bed, but can't. She groans.

He is so near she can smell his skin, cinnamon and something sharp she can't identify. "Are you okay?"

"No, I think I'm going to throw up."

He is suddenly next to her, putting an arm beneath her. "Let me help you."

"No, leave me alone." She jerks away from him, lurches towards the bathroom. She half hopes he will come and help her, but he doesn't. She feels like her guts are coming up. This will definitely make morning a more bearable experience. Wiping her mouth, she staggers out of the bathroom.

"Do you feel better?"

"I do," she says, falling into his lap. "Do you want to get it on?" She tries to put her arms around his neck, presses her breasts against his chest.

"I always found you very attractive," he says as he pries her loose.

"Past tense."

"No, it's just that I don't – "

How did he get over there, on the other bed again? She doesn't remember letting go of him. One minute he was in her arms; the next she was alone again. *Déjà vu.* "You don't what?" she asks coldly.

"I'm celibate, Jessica."

"Why? Why would you want to waste that beautiful body?"

"I try to concentrate on the spiritual realm."

She gets up, crosses the room, and falls against him, whispering in his ear, "Sex can be very spiritual."

"Please, Jessica." He pushes her gently away.

She wants to rip the shirt off his back. She wants to tear his eyes out. "Oh, Christ," she says mournfully, falling back on the bed and staring at the ceiling. "I can't believe you're rejecting me again. I can't believe I'm stupid enough to let it happen again. Do I have to be hit over the head?" She begins to beat herself on the forehead with the palm of her hand. "Stupid, stupid, stupid," she intones.

"I never rejected you. I just moved on to a different plane."

She laughs, tonelessly. "Right, one that didn't include me."

"I was afraid to tell you what was happening, afraid you'd laugh at me. But I'm secure in my position now. You could come with me."

"To your spiritual plane?"

"I'm worried about you."

"Don't be," she snaps.

"I've never seen you so drunk, or so sad."

Jessica sits up and stares at him. "Sad? Don't you pity me, you asshole. I pity you, you pathetic little spiritual ant. Don't you know there's no other plane? This is it. What you see is what you get."

"That's not true. If you could just trust me, I'd show you."

"Trust you? Trust you? You're kidding, right?"

"There is so much that needs to be done. You could help."

"Charity begins at home, motherfucker."

"Please don't talk like that."

"Oh, am I offending your sensitive ears? Poor baby." She props up the pillows behind her and sprawls again, tasting bile in her mouth.

"Look, I'm sorry I left you. I didn't think you were ready for a transformation and I needed to separate myself from all the material things that brought me down."

She doesn't even need to sit up for this one. "You sanctimonious son of a bitch," she spits, the words falling out of her mouth like the bile she can't seem to get rid of, "you left me after five years. I thought you'd run off to start a new life, but it's even worse than I imagined. You ran off to contemplate your fucking navel."

"I loved you. Truly I did. Do."

"What do you know about love?" She stands up, walks over to him, grabs his face between her hands. Forces him to look at her. "Love is not otherworldly. Love is being there. Love is sharing juices, holding my head when I throw up, tying my shoelaces when I can't bend over anymore, growing old together."

"There are many kinds of love," Daniel says, turning away from her.

"No, there's only one kind. There's the kind that puts someone else before you." She walks to the door. "That's why I'm leaving now, Daniel. Because I love you. Because I don't want to bring you down. Because I'm not good for you."

"That's not true, Jessica. Why don't you give us a chance?"

Oh, she wants to stay with him. She wants to devote her life to a noble purpose, to live free of alcohol and drugs. She wants to sleep bloodlessly beside him and wake to a clean shower and clean sheets. She wants him back.

But that is not what she says. What she says is, "Sorry, baby, I'm leaving you because I love you." How good it feels to say those words to him. It's worth it to see his face. Worth it to throw those last words he said back at him, to see that he recognizes them, to see that they hurt him so deeply, even if she's snipping off her own nose in the process. And so what if, when she gets home to her apartment, she will cry herself to sleep? For God's sake, who wants to live in Tibet anyway? It's cold.

Photographs
Colton Adrian

Cannibals

Marley Simmons Abril

Home, Spring

Bees ecstatic, the bloom brought a storm in the orchard. He snuck a round
mouse in a box into the root shed. At the pond he wet his lunch roll and
pressed small bits back into dough, offered them to new fish. His ankles
sent moons across the ruffled surface. The fish nicked his toes in the brown
water and he wondered what else the fragile world might bite. Seed nut fruit
milk cake quail goose hog. His ma spoke of God but he'd rather a stiff quill
of seeds by the cow's summer pond, new sedges in warm mud, the easy birth
of the season.

The mouse: her hot heart beat in his fingers she had a fat bare belly and
leaked out eight blind tadpoles onto a rag made of his old pants. Perplexed,
she ate them in a day.

The bees moved on to the fuchsia bed. He thinned new fruit from the
D'Anjou. The pears blushed as they grew, crowded out white petals, dragged
limbs to the dirt. He kicked the cull around the trunk. They'd rot, and make
of the tree a cannibal.

Work, Winter

At night, the freeze. His body a fist in the slump of cot. Hands on the soles
of his feet, breathing onto his knees. The men all whisper fear in their sleep,
rowed up in their tent, hot breath rising like birds to slick the canvas with ice
by dawn. In clear weather the stars describe a slide down the arc of the sky.
When cloudy, just the blunt moon and the wound of the river. He shakes as
a calf, winter-born.

The heifers put up every February in the barn to wait out their heavy time,
nostrils wide. Bulls outside with ice in their eyes. Pa's boots cracking the
snow every hour while the heifers fog clouds in the thin lantern light. From
hot belly to frosted straw they'd freeze in a minute.

Another winter: he had a sister for seventeen days. In the tintype image they are four: ma, pa, him, the girl never named. The image took three minutes and none smiled, each blink a blur. They sat still as they could but in the image the girl alone is sharp, eyes shut, fist a pebble at her chest, and them living but fogged and dim as though they were the ones leaving her behind. What God welcomes his weakest into this airless month?

Smitty
Philip St. Clair

Lunchtime in the factory breakroom, and the guy
      who reads girlie paperbacks sits in a corner
near the soda machine, locked deep into narratives
      of crash-and-burn lust or take-me-now rapture
or silk-necktie bondage, unable to react to the rattle
      when I drop in quarters for a Dr. Pepper
or the hollow clatter when the full can drops down
      through the plastic guts of the machine.
He doesn't care who sees. He ought to hide the covers
      with the shadow of his hand, or mask them
with duct tape, but there they are: naughty cheerleaders,
      submissive French maids, horny nurses,
bored housewives, all caught midway through some
      intimate, unguarded act, wearing that
wide-eyed look of surprise, lips pursed in the same
      scarlet O as they smooth nylons or brush hair
or undress for the bedroom or the bubble-bath.
      The older guys, most of them deskilled
by a flat economy, ashamed of where they have to work,
      call him names when he leaves the room:
Smutty Smitty or Smitty The Fist or just plain Jagoff.
      The younger guys just laugh. Sometimes
they invite me to Outside Storage and the narrow spaces
      between the fifteen-foot stacks of PCV pipe
where they hunker down and fire up lumpy joints
      or take turns on someone's one-hitter –
a little something to give us some edges and brights
      for the next few hours as we slouch,
half-minded, in front of our preset lathes and presses,
      knocking out nipples and elbows and tees.
Once, after the shift, I followed Smitty to the parking lot
      and watched him get into a scuffed, cluttered
Chevy Malibu. I pulled up behind him at the security gate.
      I saw him open and splay his latest paperback
across the hub of his steering wheel and I saw him read it
      as he drove, flicking his gaze from the page
to the afternoon traffic: both brake lights gone,
      the lone turn signal a fluttering broken bird.

Home Defense

Philip St. Clair

We were sitting in her living room, the lights low,
        not doing much of anything, just talking,
when her little boy marched in, eyes narrowed
        to slits, mouth twisted in hate: he never
liked me visiting his mother close to his bedtime,
        and in his right hand was a Colt 1911
forty-five automatic. I went ice-cold for a moment
        before I knew that it couldn't be real:
his mother hated firearms but she would buy
        toy ones for him – she said it would
help him come to terms with his emerging masculinity
        like football. I knew what a 1911 was.
My father kept one in his dresser, and when I was a boy
        I used to field-strip it when he was off
working his shift at the mill. It was GI issue and
        needed repair: it rattled when I shook it;
the sear was so worn that when I engaged the safety
        and squeezed the trigger the hammer fell.
My father didn't seem to care if it got fixed or not –
        it wasn't reliable and it wasn't safe.
So when she finally put her son to bed I had a chance
        to take a look – it was a full-sized model
cast in a greenish plastic that turned blue in a dim light,
        detailed down to the magazine release
and the slide stop and the plug for the recoil spring.
        I never understood why the boy chose it
over a cap gun or a squirt gun – this one couldn't
        do anything. It must have been its shape:
how easily it rides in the hand, how naturally it points.
        Perhaps it was an image from another life:
action in World War II or Korea, damage from PTSD
        lingering after. Perhaps this time around
he'll get a chance to heal himself and distance to forget.
        But I won't forget how his little shoulder
dipped in that moment I thought he was armed: a 1911
        loaded with hardball weighs three pounds.

Snow
Claudia Serea

Snow falls everywhere all the time,
especially in far-away places,
like Eastern Europe,
Africa, or Thailand.

We trail the blizzard with us,
a cape covering continents.

Snow falls over the city,
over gray buildings, cars, and noise.

White noise,
snow falls between us,
curtains, walls,
and mountains fall.

Snow falls on your coat,
in your hair and eyelashes.

When we speak,
snowflakes get in our mouths.

It snows inside us, until
we fill with silence.

Now let's make snow angels
inside each other.

Summer Rain at the End of October

Claudia Serea

Liquid bulls run through the city.

It hasn't rained all summer,
and now, even with an umbrella,
I still get soaked.

Cars honk,
people crowd
under scaffoldings and eaves,
babies cry in their strollers,

and the rain,
the rain gets louder,
white-gray,
furious hooves.

In flats and skinny jeans,
the city girls pass by
with their phones
and selfie drawl,
cat eyes
and messy buns.

And the rain,
the rain falls harder,
thunderous,
frothy bulls.

There's no way I'll walk now,

so I'll stand here,
under this sliver of an awning,
eat a slice of pizza,

and wait.

Beets
Claudia Serea

My hands were red and raw from the cold
like the tiny discarded beets
left behind the long-gone tractors.

At nightfall, crimson juices
smeared the November sky.

No one saw us stealing
from the cold ground.
Only the starlings and crows.

No one saw the small hands
digging into the dirt,
feeling for round roots
sweet like candy.

Boiled, the beets were soft
and bloodied our mouths

as if we ate the sun.

Wednesday Morning
Claudia Serea

Another one of these
sunny days

with a gray pigeon stranded
in the sky,

with too much Facebooking
and not enough reading,

too much need
and not enough want,

and the sharp memory
of mountains or clouds

cut out of blue
cellophane.

In the Other Room
Claudia Serea

No one would notice I'm not there,
captivated as they are
by their TV, YouTube,
Facebook and Snapchat friends.

I could be gone for hours,
for days,

if I'd take the barely visible path
through the trees,
and walk into the deep green far enough
to make it hard
to come back.

And they would still be shopping,
watching, chatting online—
Who, Mom?
She's just
in the other room.

But I'd be gone.

I'd float down the river until
I'd reach the ocean,

a stitch
on the horizon seam.

The sky is high,
the world is wide,

and no one would know I'm gone.

Making Chairs
Tim Nalley

The serrated edge of the bread knife left little scars along the baloney. I sliced it thin, not thick like my father used to like it, but as thin as I could get it without making holes. When the skillet was hot, I placed the meat scarred side down and listened to the sizzle and pop as the processed meat started to caramelize. The center rose and made a little dome—the very reason I'd always liked it sliced thin. The thick baloney wouldn't bubble up in the middle. I poked the center with a knife and watched the cloud of smoke escape then flipped the baloney to the other side and placed a slice of Colby cheese on top of it. I laid two pieces of bread on a Styrofoam plate and slabbed a big glob of mayonnaise on both slices. When the baloney was done—the sweetish smell of the seared meat the indicator—I placed it and the cheese on my sandwich.

Through the window above the sink, I could see the snow beginning to thicken over the back yard. It very rarely snowed in Alabama, but when it did, I always craved fried baloney. I was only about ten in the blizzard of '93, but I remembered making fried baloney sandwiches with my dad for lunch every day we were snowed in. Every day we would make those sandwiches. Dad would make an extra for mom, and when I'd take it to her, she would smile and say "thank you," and eat it slowly. I knew she didn't like baloney, but she didn't complain at all that week we were snowed in, just smiled and thanked me and ate the sandwich. I think it was because she was happy to have Dad home to make the sandwiches for her.

The day my dad came home from Desert Storm, Mom was antsy. She kept reaching for her neck and playing with her hair in the rearview mirror of the truck on the way to the airport. I'd never seen her obsess so much over her appearance, but every few minutes, she looked in the mirror and ran her hands through her hair. The sky was the color of coal. When we got close to Birmingham, the rain came gushing down. We waited for about an hour for his plane to come in, and every few minutes, she would run over to the window to look at the planes that were arriving like she would be able to see him. If she wasn't running for the windows, she was fussing over her hair, and cussing the rain for making it fall. When he finally arrived, she ran to him and jumped in his arms. It was like all of those romantic tearjerkers she was always watching. In the truck, Mama wanted to sit in the middle, which I thought was odd, but I didn't argue because I was usually stuck in the middle and I was happy to be able to sit by the window. All the way home, she sat with her arms around his waist while he drove. I thought he looked uncomfortable, but if he was, he never said a word about it.

Before the war, Daddy had made his living making and selling wooden chairs, and since he'd come home, he was right back at it. He didn't use processed lumber. Instead he'd wake up early in the morning and forage for twigs and branches in the woods behind our house, then he'd spend the rest of the morning and early afternoon in his shop. We could hear him cutting and hammering all day. Then in the late afternoon, he would make his deliveries. He traveled all over Saint Clair, and Shelby, and Jefferson county, delivering chairs and tables to all manner of people. On Sundays, we'd all pile in his truck to head to church, and then he'd be right back in that shop when he got home. He was always making furniture, always delivering, so I knew he must have been making a good living at it.

Every now and then, Mama would go out and sit on an old stump he'd made for her before the war. She'd go on and on about her day or about the gossip of the town; about so-and-so's new boyfriend or such-and-such's financial woes. Before the war she was out there near every day, but since he came home she was sitting on that stump less and less.

He wouldn't let me come in the shop, but he'd leave the door open so I could watch him work. I would watch him shape the legs, measuring them even, bending and forcing them where he wanted them to be. He'd sand the feet until they were flat. After he got the stretcher on, he'd sit in it to make sure it was all even, and every time it was just about perfect. I never saw him have to cut any off after he'd got it all together.

One Friday after school, Daddy met me in the driveway in his truck. "Hop in," he said. Mama was standing on the porch waving at me. I waved back and threw my backpack in the back of the truck, climbed in. We drove a piece, crossed over Logan Martin and past a couple of farms that were bunched up together near Vincent until we got to a small trailer on a bunch of land off Highway 25. There were goats out front and a chicken coop off to the side. The trailer looked like it was in need of a good pressure washing, and the yard stunk of chicken and goat shit. "Stay here," daddy said, and he climbed out of the truck and grabbed the lone chair out of the back. I watched him through the rear window approach the porch and knock. An older black man answered. They talked for a minute, and I noticed the longer they talked the more my daddy started waving his finger and pointing at the guy, stabbing the point of his finger into the guys chest. His voice kept getting louder. The guy held up his hands and waved Daddy off, went to walk back inside, but Daddy grabbed him and pulled him back out. After that, everything went a little crazy. The guy reached in the back of his pants and pulled out a pistol, went to point it at Daddy, but Daddy grabbed his hand. He pinned him against the wall while he wrestled the pistol away from him. I just sat in the truck, frozen. Daddy moved with a violence I'd never seen before.

After he got the pistol away, he flung the guy down on the chair. When he hit it, I noticed a wrapped up package fell from the bottom of the chair on top of him. Daddy mounted him and kept punching him over and over in the face. I opened the door of the truck, and it made a loud squeak. He looked over at me, blood spattered on his chin, his eyes wild like I'd never seen them. It scared me. He still had that pistol in his hand. I wondered for a second if he was going to shoot that man, but he didn't. He threw it at him, but the guy didn't move. I wondered if he was dead.

Daddy didn't say anything when he got back in the truck. He grabbed a towel from behind his seat and wiped the blood off his hands and his face. I watched the black man lying there on the porch through the rear window as we pulled out of the driveway. He never moved in the time it took us to get from the house to 25. When we got far enough away I couldn't see him anymore, I turned back around. "Is he dead," I asked him.

"Nah. He ain't dead." He looked at me for a minute and his face started to soften.

One night before he went to Iraq—I couldn't have been more than six—we were sitting down to dinner and everything was real quiet, and he said, "Did y'all hear about that fight at the Captain D's last night?" Mama and I both shook our heads. "I don't know if it was a biker gang or what, but it was brutal." He paused for a minute, waiting for the perfect time to deliver his punchline. Whenever the joke was especially corny, his lip would always curl up on the right side in a sort of half-smile, trying not to give it away. "Every single fish in that place was battered," he said, and then he was banging on the table laughing while Mama and I shook our heads and groaned. "Every fish was battered, Eamon," he yelled. Me and Mama couldn't help but laugh after that. Since he came home, though, I couldn't even remember seeing him so much as cracking a smile.

We got back into town and he pulled off at Smith's and came out a few minutes later with a six-pack of Coors. He drank a few of them there in the truck and tucked the other two behind the seat. "You ever been in a fight?" he asked.

I shook my head.

"Don't ever start a fight, but if somebody comes at you, you by God defend yourself. You understand?"

I nodded and he grabbed me by the neck and pulled me over to him and gave me a rough hug. "Maybe tomorrow I can teach you to scrap." He laughed and started the truck up. For a second, that laugh reminded me of the way he was before the war, those corny dad jokes and that big guffaw. When we pulled up in the driveway a few minutes later, though, it was gone. I went to get out of the truck and he grabbed me by my shirt. "Best your mama doesn't hear about this."

"Yes sir," I said.

◆

Mama and I were sitting on the couch watching *Tom and Jerry* the next morning when Daddy came in. As soon as he walked in the room, Mama moved to the kitchen, grabbed a rag off the sink, and started wiping the counters. Daddy didn't say anything to her. He just watched her. They were like that more and more the longer he'd been home. She seemed like a completely different person from the woman who held on to him all the way home from the airport just a couple of weeks before. Now they were like ghosts haunting the same house, moving from room to room, and never meeting in between. After a few seconds, he looked back at me. "Come on. I wanna show you something," he said.

I followed him out to the shop where he pointed at Mama's stump. "Sit," he said. He grabbed a clamp off his table. His workspace was even emptier and cleaner than our dinner table. He held the clamp up, spun the handle. "Know what this is he asked.

"It's a clamp," I said.

"C-clamp." He grabbed a few twigs and used the c-clamp to hold them together.

I looked around the shop. Everything had a place, and everything was exactly where it should have been. On the wall behind him hung peg-board with tools—hammers, clamps, pliers, and saws—in various shapes and sizes. One spot sat empty with the shape of the clamp Daddy was holding drawn perfectly in permanent marker. What I loved the most, though, was the smell, like what I would imagine a Christmas tree farm to smell like; the smell of whittling a point on the end of a stick, but multiplied by a hundred.

He grabbed a piece of twine and used it to bind the twigs together. "Watch everything I do," he said. As he hammered a nail into the branches, he kept moving his fingers farther and farther from the impact point. He seemed almost afraid of the hammer coming down on his finger. I'd never seen him like that. Afraid. He was always a little wild and never really showed fear of anything. Once, when we were fishing, I saw him grab a moccasin by the tail without even flinching. He was always doing stuff like that. But that day in his shop he looked vulnerable. Like he was thinking of all the crazy things he'd done over his life and wondering how he hadn't died and what crazy thing he might do that would finally beat him. He wouldn't let me touch any of the saws or clippers. He was even a little timid with them. More than anything, though, he wanted me to watch. He just kept saying, "I'm not always going to be around." And I remember his eyes were wide. Wider than I'd ever seen anyone's eyes, and he kept looking all around like he was afraid that at any time, someone or something might come out from under a table or something.

After he put a chair together, he made me follow him outside. In the driveway, he squatted down. "I want you to punch me," he said.

I just stared at him. I didn't want to hit him. Hell, I didn't want to hit anybody. There were boys at school that would sooner hit you than look at you, but those boys were the kind of boys I didn't want anything to do with. One of them, Rex, was always trying to pick a fight with me when I was minding my own business reading a book in the lunchroom. Just a couple of days before he'd come over and knocked my tray to the floor and when I bent to pick it up, he drove his knee into the back of my head.

"I need to know what I'm working with, boy. Punch me."

I knew he wouldn't stop until I did what he said, so I balled my fist up and tried to put my full force behind the punch. Daddy staggered back a bit, but he didn't fall. He shook his head. "Shit," he said. "Hit me, dammit."

It was cold that day. One of the coldest of the winter. He made me stay out there with him until I could hit him hard enough to knock him back. He taught me to go for the knees and try to take the guy down. I remember leaning over him after he'd showed me how to take him down feeling his heavy breath in my face, smelling the beer on his breath. "If you get a guy on the

Illustration by Stephen Smith

ground," he said. "You can pound on his face as much as you want. It don't matter how wimpy your punches are then. But if all else fails, you need to know how to shoot." He pulled a pistol out of his waistband. "This here's a Beretta 92FS," he said. "Just like the M9 I carried in the war."

I stared at the gun. I knew he carried. He used to take me down to South Sandy to shoot before the war, but it still scared me seeing him with it. He held it out to me. "Take it," he said. I hesitated for a second, but took it from him. I tried to remember everything he had taught me about holding it. Finger on the guard, never on the trigger, pointed at the ground. "You handle that thing pretty good," he said. "I want you to point it at me."

I held the gun at my side and stared at him, dumbfounded by what he'd just said.

"Now it's loaded, so you keep your finger off the trigger, but I want you to get the feel for what it's like to point a gun at somebody."

"I can't," I said.

"Don't be a pussy, Eamon. You hit like a god damn vegetarian, and I need to know you can defend yourself if it comes down to it."

I held it at my side for a little longer, feeling the weight of it in my hands, then I lifted it to his chest for half a second and quickly let it drop back to my side.

"Not like that," he said. "Hold it like I taught you. Like you aim to let that bullet fly."

"I can't, Daddy," I said.

"Goddammit, son. Do what I say." I jumped when he raised his voice. I'd never heard that tone from him before. "Obey me," he said.

I moved my feet to stand in the isosceles stance like he'd shown me, held the gun up to his chest. I lined the sights up right in the middle.

"Good," he said. "Hold it there for a minute. Get a feel for it. I want you to tell yourself you could pull that trigger if you ever had to. Let me hear you say it."

I said nothing. Just stood there barely able to keep the gun up from trembling.

"Say it, boy."

"I could pull the trigger," I said.

"Say it again."

"I could pull the trigger."

He moved off to the side and came over and took the gun from me. I was shaking, but I didn't know if it was more from the cold or from pointing a loaded pistol at my father. My toes and fingers stung with frostbite, but I barely even noticed the pain.

Mama was sitting on the sofa when we got back inside. I sat next to her, still shivering. She grabbed my hand, shook her head at Daddy when she saw the red of my knuckles, but other than that she didn't raise any objections. "I've done ate," she said. "Y'all can make yourselves a baloney." She didn't look at either of us when she said it. She just kept watching some show about wedding dresses.

◆

A few nights after that, Daddy came stumbling into my room in the middle of the night. He'd been out delivering when I came home from school. His eyes were bloodshot and he was shaking. He looked like a different man, a man I didn't recognize. He didn't say anything when he walked in. He just sat in the floor next to my bed for a while, staring out the window.

I woke the next morning to sirens blaring coming up our driveway. I ran outside to see them cuffing him and loading him in the back of the car. Mama was screaming and trying to get away from one of the officers holding her back. I just stared at him. I couldn't stop thinking about him making me point that gun at him.

After they left, Mama just sat on the porch screaming and begging for him to come back.

At school the next day, Rex came up and tripped me. He stood over me, holding me down with his foot "Your daddy's a coward," he said. "And a fucking psycho killer."

"Get off me, asshole," I shot back.

"What you gonna do," he said. "Shoot me like your daddy did that old man?"

"Shut up."

"Or you gonna run away like your daddy did from the war."

Before I even knew what was happening, I tackled him at the knees, pinning him to the ground. I dropped my fist on his nose, putting every bit of my weight behind it that I could muster. I punched him two or three times before the blood started trickling out. Seeing it, I froze there, suddenly afraid of how easy it had been for me to make another boy bleed. I let him up and he ran away.

"How was your day," Mama asked when I got home.

"Good," I said. I knew I didn't need to tell her about the fight. The school would call her if they hadn't already and I knew she was still too hung up on Daddy to even care. I walked out to the shop, pulled the c-clamp off the wall, and sat on the stump, staring at everything in its place, just as he left it, and just as he would have wanted it to stay. Then I threw the clamp against the pegboard wall, watched the tools scatter and fall to the floor, and walked inside to make myself a fried baloney.

I sliced it thin, not thick like my father liked it, but as thin as I could get it without making holes.

Rammer Jammer

Ashley M. Jones

George Wallace Stands in the
Schoolhouse Door -June 11, 1963

Between the thighs
of the doorway,
you are powerful.
The confetti of camera clicks
and your smart business suit
and the swamp of teenaged protesters
swaddle you with sweat.
June in Alabama is rife with heat.
Important men
from Washington have come
to clear you out.
Tension,
thick and bitter
as a watermelon rind.
From the doorway,
you see Vivian and James
waiting in the government car.
They wish to register here.
From the doorway,
you see walls and waves of
ballot-faced whites.
They are checkmarks
in the next election.
It is only after
your speech is delivered
that you realize how thirsty you are—
your cottonmouth
is unbecoming
for a state leader.

How nice it would be
to sit on your porch
with Lurleen and a glass of sweet tea.
How nice it would be
to get out of this heat
and out of Tuscaloosa
and back to marbled Montgomery
and its halls that echo—
obedient, loud, and white.

So Far Away

Regan Green

Wells had decided to quit drinking again since his wife Willy got pregnant. Or rather—she had decided that Wells had decided to quit drinking again. Which meant that I got to drink all their beer when I was over at their house early mornings before we went dove hunting or nights like Friday night, sitting on the porch. We were listening to Blood on the Tracks and—at Willy's demand—some sissy sentimental crap by Carole King or somebody. Finally Wells had grown tired of the lovesick ballads and said that he was gonna drive me to town to get some cigarettes, which was what we always said when we grew tired of Willy's lovesick ballads.

"More cigarettes, Wink?" She looked at me hard.

"Yes'm."

She popped her gum hard. "Didn't you boys get you some cigarettes yesterday?"

"Yes'm. I reckon we did."

She blew out her breath hard and turned to Wells. "None for you, you hear? You can smoke when your sons are old enough to move out, but I don't want Julius and Reuben and Baby Gus growin up to be like their daddy."

He didn't say anything. Just narrowed his eyes and looked past my shoulder.

"You hear me?"

"I hear you, woman."

I've never been married, so I don't know much about it. But it's always seemed to me that those two must have been delusional or desperate or shitfaced to have ended up in such an unholy matrimony. I imagined how it happened sometimes. When we were all sitting on their porch after Wells and I got off work at Crosby & Crosby A/C, we sat in silence. Everything slowed down and the pain in our backs numbed and the sweat on our chests dripped down until all the drops pooled in the folds of fat above our bellies. On those nights, I looked at my brother's face, and then at his wife's, and I imagined why they got married nine years, three sons, and two shattered Carole King records ago.

Some nights I imagined they got married because their names start with the same letter—Wells and Willy.

Some nights I imagined they both had some awful kinky fetish that no one else would oblige.

Some nights I imagined before she met my brother, she was in a marriage of bipolarity and beatings, so when she finally shot that man with his own Colt M1911, she sought out a loveless man who would never love her or beat her.

Some nights I thought it was just because her head fit right under his chin when they hugged and because they both liked that cheap Yuengling Beer—it reminded him of our dad and her of college. And because they were both Presbyterians but not upstanding Presbyterians.

"Come on, Wink, let's get you some Newports."

Wells and I hopped into his truck and slapped in the Moondance cassette and started down the road. We listened for a few minutes. The road was grainy and loud. The headlights shone onto the milky fog but not through it. I pointed out the house of Delaney Piper, that fairy-faced girl and teased Wells for liking her in grade school and he told me to fuck off. We silently passed the snake-handling church with no windows and a deer ran out in front of the truck and we missed it by a jackrabbit hair, Wells screaming, and then we were quiet til the tacky purple sofa rose in the headlights.

Wells stopped the truck and whispered, "Goddamn," with more reverence than I had ever heard him use in singing the doxology in church. He got out of the truck.

I gulped down the last of the Yuengling, tossed the can out the window, and followed him. At first I tried to tell myself it wasn't the same one, it wasn't ours. But then I saw the burn holes along the top of the back cushion—she used to like to hang her arm behind her head, forgetting she had one of my Newports between her fingers, leaving awful stains and the smell of smoke and perfume in the threads. God, I missed that perfume. I missed the way it tasted like peppered honeysuckle on her thighs. I missed the thin varnish it left over her skin in the mornings before it dried into the tiny hairs on the back of her neck. Like dew drying into the ground.

I made her take the sofa with her when she left and told her it was because I hated that tacky purple velvet. But it was because I couldn't stand seeing it under my roof because I still loved her and we both knew it.

"It's not purple," she'd said. "It's boysenberry."

I wish she hadn't said that, because it ruined boysenberry jam for me. Thank God we didn't have a beer-colored sofa.

I guess she'd dumped it out there, where she knew I'd be sooner or later, the road to Mackey Donn's grocery where I got half off my cigarette packs for keeping quiet about Mack hunting out of season. And I guess that meant she'd got a new guy. And I guess he'd probably stayed over one night and said, "Where'd you get this shit sofa," and she'd probably said, "From a shit guy," and they'd probably said at the same time, "Let's get rid of it."

I curled up on the sofa and pressed my face into the matted velvet. It still smelled like her. Like red—"vermillion," she'd say—oil pastel smudges under fingernails and dew on musty firewood in the morning and Creedence records. I don't know why, but Creedence records smell different than other records. And it smelled of something else, a beer—but not mine. Corona, I think. I guess he was a Corona man. I stayed there, curled into the corner of that shit sofa, and Wells didn't try to stop me. He just looked away and picked at his ears.

After a while, he sighed and drove off in his truck and when he came back he had a bottle of Jack and a pack of Newports in hand. He put them on the ground beside me. I rolled onto my side to take a swig of the jack and when I spilled some of it, he turned away so he couldn't see it run down my chin onto the cushions. I set it down on the ground and he sat there a while, long legs straddling the sofa arm.

"You gonna stay here?"

I didn't answer.

"We oughta go home."

"I am home." My voice was muffled in the mossy fabric.

"Let me take you home."

"I am home."

"You're better than this, Wink."

"You're wrong."

He left after that. And Willy probably said, "How come little duckling brother isn't shuffling behind you?" and Wells probably said, "Shut up, woman," and she probably said, "It's about time he quit following you home." And Wells probably didn't say anything.

I rolled onto my back and pushed my hands over my face and through my hair and breathed in the clean, cold air and there were the stars above me and Betelgeuse sparkling blue—"Egyptian blue"—and all the constellations she had taught me. I spent a lot of mornings beside her on this sofa with my head in her lap while she read Hemingway and I pretended to read Steinbeck.

And I spent a lot of afternoons sitting like Indians with her on this sofa playing cards—mostly gin rummy, because she always won. And I spent a lot of nights stretched out on the sofa with my arm around, watching the pearl white light of the television blink on her face in the darkness and thinking that if I bit into her, she would bleed peach juice syrupy and amber-colored instead of blood. And then at the end, I spent a lot of nights trying to go to sleep on the sofa by myself, picking stray strands of her long, black hair off the velvet.

Some of the stuffing was coming out of a hole in the cushion beside me and I began drunkenly fidgeting with it between hiccups, holding my lighter to it so the fibers glowed bright red—"poppy red"—until it burned out and smelled like her hair after she'd left it wrapped around a curling iron too long. I fiddled with it and then I jerked at it and then I tore at it until I had gathered a big enough chunk that it didn't burn out, and the glowing fibers became a small flame and the small flame spread over the skin of the sofa until the whole thing was lit up. I rolled off the sofa, snatched up the bottle, and shuffled back. The wilting cushions caught fire quick but the arms and legs took longer to burn, and rosy embers jumped and arched away from it like willow tree branches. It was kinda pretty. I picked a cigarette out of my back pocket, held it out and lit it with the flames, and took a long drag.

I wondered if her head fit right under his chin. And if he drank that Barefoot Wine she liked. And if he was a half-hearted Catholic like her.

Or maybe it was because their names start with the same letter. Which would mean his name is Sherwin or Shephard or Shawn or something like that.

Shiloh and Shawn. Whoever.

Sounds a hell of a lot better than Shiloh and Wink.

How to Do Nothing
Robert Okaji

First you must wash the window to observe more clearly
the dandelion seed heads bobbing in the wind. Next,

announce on Facebook and Twitter that you will be offline
for the next two days, if not forever. Heat water for tea.

Remember the bill you forgot to pay, and then cleanse
your mind of all regret. Consider industrial solvents

and the smoothness of sand-scoured stone, the miracle
of erasure. Eliminate all thought, but remember

the water. Hitch a ride on a Miles Davis solo and float
away on a raft of bluesy notes and lions' teeth,

and wonder how to sabotage your neighbor's leaf blower,
but nicely, of course. She's a widow with a gun.

Now it is time to empty yourself. Close your eyes.
Become a single drop of dew on a constellation of petals.

Evaporate, share the bliss. Stuff that dog's bark
into a lock box alongside the tapping at the door,

the phone's vibration, the neighbor's rumbling bass,
and the nagging, forgotten something that won't

solidify until three in the morning, keeping you awake.
But don't ignore the whistling. You must steep the tea.

And All Around, the Withered

Robert Okaji

I total the numbers printed
on passing boxcars,

multiply by seven, then add two,
subtracting every third odd number,

only to find, in the end, myself
tethered to this empty platform,

spelling hapless with integers,
acknowledging Zahlen and

the infinite. Sometimes gravel, too,
calls to me and I observe space

in the path's patterns, constellation
stacked upon constellation,

multi-dimensional galaxies
expanding in one swooping arc,

heroic eagles and exploding stars
complicit in their deeds and forever

locked in sequence, yet when I explain
my vision, the words emerge

as convex polyhedrons or inverted,
drooled gasps, and people turn aside.

That boy's two bricks shy a full load, they
say. The lights are on but nobody's home.

Orbit
Ellen Perry

"Perhaps if Death is kind, and there can be returning,
We will come back to earth some fragrant night,
And take these lanes to find the sea, and bending
Breathe the same honeysuckle, low and white.

We will come down at night to these resounding beaches
And the long gentle thunder of the sea,
Here for a single hour in the wide starlight
We shall be happy, for the dead are free."

Sara Teasdale, "If Death Is Kind" (1920)

On the Tuesday after the Friday when Iris had her blood drawn, down at the Angels of Mercy Lab Express, her mother Francine called. Iris wouldn't dare address her mother by her first name, but in retelling various episodes to her friends over the years, Iris always used "Francine."

"Did you ever find out whether you'd had a stroke or not?" Francine asked, not even bothering to say hello.

Iris sighed. "No, Mom, they haven't called with any results yet."

"I'm betting it was a stroke, a mild stroke. Nothing to worry about. Because they've caught it early."

"Mom," Iris said, "If it was a stroke, it already happened. They can't catch something early that already happened."

"Well, you know, the doctors can counterdict the effects of it, probably."

"*Contradict*," Iris corrected, though *contradict* didn't seem quite right either. In any case, her mother ignored the correction and Iris decided let it go—mostly because she had no choice, since Francine went right on with her declaration.

"Yeah, I bet they can fix that droopiness in no time flat since it's just on the one side. Well, I've got to see to the clothesline while the sun's out. Call me when they tell you what we can do about the stroke."

Iris never got used to the way her mother, for all of Francine's interest in Southern manners, just hung up the phone without ending conversations properly. No polite "bye-bye" or casually-friendly "see you later" for Francine. Iris sighed, thought about how frequently she sighed these days, put her phone on silent, and looked around her living room from the vantage point of the old rocking chair she'd bought for her first college apartment. There were photographs perfectly placed on the mantel, by the lamps, near a window overlooking her neighbor's garden. Iris stood up and gazed with fresh eyes into the bright faces of her nieces and nephews, departed grandparents, friends from the neighborhood, friends from work, former students all grown up and married with children and jobs and dogs and mortgages. Iris wondered: were these people alive in the pictures? Had they been truly alive when the cameras flashed, and were they still living right there in her living room even if they were no longer on the planet?

As a middle school science teacher, Iris had thought a lot about other planets, the universe, various galaxies, and more and more lately that they didn't seem to know or care about Earth. Nearing retirement now, Iris looked back on her life almost daily, a frequent impulse that, like sighing, had begun to alarm her. In kindergarten she'd announced that she wanted to be an astronaut; in those days, she thought about space in a dreamy, thrilling, childlike way. What could be out there? Anything! Everything. She could explore the possibilities and float on a magic carpet and battle mean black holes, and people back home on little Earth and even tinier Memphis would listen on TV to what she had to say about it. Years passed and Iris's passion remained true. Her high school counselor talked to her about a career in Astrophysics. She was primed for great discovery, financial success, and cosmic adventure most of all. What had happened? Who was it said something about how we can only understand life backwards but have to live it forwards?

When Iris took a first-year astronomy course in college, sharp terror replaced eager anticipation and desire. What was out there? Nothing. Everything. Mostly nothing. The dread of existence, nothingness, and the brevity of human life was so severe that by her sophomore year Iris decided to go the safe route: stick to the
basics, earn her license to teach in the state of Tennessee, and try to get kids interested in rocks and soil, leaves and plants—everything that was firmly grounded. She left space alone and, in return, the dark void didn't say much to her about it one way or the other.

The void left Iris alone, that is, until as an exhausted 50-something middle school teacher she felt the empty space tugging at her with icy fingers while she made the rounds at various doctors' offices. "Hm," the white-coated professionals said, looking in her eyes and listening to her chest. "Hm." Iris couldn't describe what was wrong; her cheek was swollen a little and her right eye had lost some muscle tone—"as we get older, that happens," one perky young doctor proclaimed, smiling—but there was a brokenness in Iris that seemed beyond fixing, past help, and she didn't know what to do about it except agree to have her blood drawn after the school year was over, see what might show up.

"Well, nothing showed up," Iris said to Francine when her mother stopped by Iris's house with some tuna salad—"You need some protean what with this fixation on not eating hamburgers anymore. What's that all about, anyway?" Francine said, mispronouncing "protein" for the hundredth time. Iris was about to explain her concerns related to beef consumption but Francine had already moved along in her mind. Besides, Iris didn't have the strength; it was late June and the Memphis heat had made its way to the suburbs and onto the front porch.

"Nothing showed up, you say. What in the world?" Francine exclaimed. "They must've missed something. Listen, we need to get inside, Iris. This sun isn't good for your skin. Did you ask them to check out that mole while you were in there?"

"The blood work people don't look at moles."

"I'm worried it's the cancer. Kind of got those irregular borders Dr. Oz and them are always talking about." Francine leaned in to scrutinize the had-to-be-malignant mole on Iris's chin. "Oh, that reminds me. You don't need to be going to the beach, for one because of all the drunks on the highway down there in Alabama, and for two because of the cancer."

Iris shook her head, thinking about her 4th of July weekend beach trip with some girlfriends who had all backed out at the last minute: sick parent, sick grandchild, distant kin coming in, husband can't get off work and needs help managing distant kin, deadlines at the office, not enough time, not enough money. Funny thing was, Iris had complete space and freedom in that space: no kids, no husband, no work in the summer, and money she'd squirreled away. She could go off and explore on her own, just as she'd imagined her life would be when she was a child. What kept holding her back? The empty space settled in around Iris's heart, mocked her in a way that brought on a little chill despite the muggy heat beating down on her herb garden.

"Well, don't worry about it," Iris sighed. "We're going to cancel the trip. Aileen bought travel insurance. Got a few days to do it."

"Good," Francine said. "That's what your daddy says, always smart to have an out. You can stay here and we'll go to some flea markets, or see about that mole, or something."

Or something.

Iris was frozen as she watched her mother drive away, overcome with a sort of reverse-terror: now she was afraid of not having *enough* space, of drawing into herself the way a rocket might get sucked into a black hole, never to be heard from again. In college she flailed and drowned in ever-expanding galaxies; now, Iris had become a lone ice-rock ring with no hope of connecting with the planet she encircled. How had she initiated this orbit?

It started, Iris realized, when her husband died. Well, Ward didn't really die; he left one day in early January when Iris was out back taking down Christmas lights, but that was the same thing, really. Leaving is dying; the grief is the same, maybe worse. Ward moved to Tunica and she only heard from him when he wanted to mention a few things he forgot: the mower bag, a can of oil, work gloves, the ring he'd given her because, well, he'd heard she was still wearing it and that could be embarrassing for both of them, especially now that he had Mandy. Iris met Ward at a Starbucks parking lot that February with everything in a shopping bag and, after the hand-off, they never spoke again. So, really, he died. And she had, too, at age 33 when it happened. "It is finished," Jesus himself said, forsaken, and the thunder rolled.

Iris didn't go to church anymore but she sure believed in scientific regeneration, in evolution, in the cycles of nature. Francine called it Christ's miraculous resurrection. Three days! "Only three days from despair to victory," Francine liked to remind everyone. Iris had three days before the deadline to cancel the trip. Dare she go alone? What if a drunk man knocked her down on the boardwalk and took her credit cards? What if the sun really did her in this time, amped up the cancer on her chin leading the doctor to inevitably boom upon her return, "YOU HAVE THREE MONTHS TO LIVE!"?

You know what happened to Tabitha, Iris: the surgeon opened her up, took one look in there, and sewed her back up again, nothing to be done.

These voices, mostly her mother's, kept Iris in fear. The heartache, mostly due to her ex-husband's betrayal, kept Iris in grief and chronic states of vague illness.

Enough. She decided to drive down to the coast on her own, maybe even drink margaritas and read some poetry while lying in a hammock on the white sand. Her niece Daniela, an English major, had given her a book of poems by Sara Teasdale that she might take along. There was one poem Iris liked—especially on those days when she longed to die—about the kindness of Death, the mercy of it, the freedom it promised. But now Iris turned the meaning around, just as she had done with her thoughts about space. She had surely endured a living death for long enough; now, with a clean bill of health, she was ready to leap off her icy orbit into the warmth of life. The salty ocean was the best place for such a rebirth.

"Mom, will you and Dad water my plants while I'm at Gulf Shores?" Iris asked Francine over the phone. Listening to the frantic questioning voices on the other end, first Francine's and then her father's, Iris rummaged in the back of her closet trying to find that old suitcase she'd taken on her honeymoon, lifetimes ago.

"No, I sure don't, Mom," Iris answered, smiling, heart pounding. "I don't know how long I'll be gone."

Demons on the Clothesline
Len Kuntz

All my other selves are hanging on the clothesline
The thin ones, the sour, the sin-stained,
The bloody awful red ones
The sun looks away and the wind screeches to a halt
A pair of children wonder what to make of it
Raising a tree branch they treat me like a piñata
When nothing falls, they get a can of gasoline
And spritz my feet and calves, light a match
As the flames lick, I smolder black and tarry
There is no tortured screaming
I watch it all, sighing, thinking perhaps
It is finished

Shattered
Len Kuntz

Your allergies are acting up again
It's the pollen or the way the water warps
In the drinking glass you shatter in the sink
Meds can take the edge off, smooth a few sharp corners
But there are days and nights when volcanoes spew
Their lava down your throat and suffocation
Seems like a very real possibility
So under the bridge you go
The sound of the cars overhead a kind of
Auditory waterboarding
Peace is a slippery distance
And the demons are never satiated
If you could just come home
If we could just talk for once
Like father and son
Or friend to friend
We might forge a footprint
Cut down the weeds and detritus
And carve a way back to the beginning

Somnambulism
Len Kuntz

Alone again, you find yourself without ribs
Your heart hanging loose by a bloody tendril
The moon mocks you while
Stars form a bejeweled noose
You hear your mother's ancient instruction
This is how we pick ourselves up
And so you walk to the window
To the lake
To the shore
Where the water accepts you as you are
Because what other choice does it have?
You float in an uneven eddy
Twirling in stilted patterns
Moonbeams striping your face
While galaxies expand for no other reason than
That they can
Seconds pass, minutes, too
And you as well
One with the unsteady current
A soggy carcass never so sad
Hoping to float to a new world
Where things bloom and can be resurrected

Sole

Diane Thomas-Plunk

If it hadn't been for Daddy's sickness, Opal Pratt might have worked a lifetime at the shoe factory no matter what had happened there.

It probably started at Opal's high school graduation. Two of her mother's sisters, three of her father's brothers and one of his sisters, their spouses, and assorted, slow-witted cousins arrived to celebrate her accomplishment. She was the first from both sides of the family to graduate from high school. The aunts hoped she would be an inspiration to their broods. The uncles only hoped their brats would go to work.

After the ceremony, they all gathered at the Pratt's modest home. Daddy had dug a pit and was barbecuing a goat with the help of the uncles and several beers. Momma boiled roasting ears and cooked snap peas with hog fat. Aunt Bella worked the churn for peach ice cream from the fruit she'd brought down from Ripley.

◆

Opal took additional helpings of ice and rock salt to Aunt Bella and spelled her working the crank. It was hard work.

"You've done a good thing, Opal girl. You got your diploma and you're goin' to work Monday. You're a good girl and you always make us proud. You always *will* make us proud, won't you?"

Opal wasn't sure if it was a question or command, but she said "Yes, ma'am" and kept churning. The whole family was proud of her, and she felt like a star.

Opal was relieved to be free of school. She had not been an honor roll student. On the other hand, she'd never been held back. She didn't run in the cheerleader/jock crowd, but she wasn't one of the redneck bunch either. She'd managed to slide through school almost invisibly. Sometimes she wondered if she really existed.

For four days after graduation, Opal luxuriated with no lessons to worry over. She accomplished her daily chores, listened to the radio and daydreamed about her future. On Monday, her world would change.

Daddy never had much to say, but on that Monday morning when Opal climbed into the truck's cab with him, he practically made a speech.

"I got you this job, girlie, and it's on my head if you muck it up. I'll be retiring soon, and I aim to go with my head held high. Do what the bosses tell you. Be respectful. Don't shame me."

"I'd never shame you, Daddy."

And that was her promise.

Daddy left her with Mrs. Blaylock, secretary to the big boss, and Opal's supervisor. She called Opal a clerical helper and showed her to the workroom where Opal was to do most of her tasks. A large worktable dominated the center of the room.

Paper, envelopes, pencils, pens, paper clips and items she didn't recognize lined shelves across one wall. A mimeograph machine sat at the end of the big table. Opal must learn to operate it. Mail was delivered to the workroom, and Opal would sort and deliver it to the right people. She could barely remember all the instructions and was sure that opportunities abounded for mistakes that would let down Daddy.

There were two lesser managers working for the big boss in the office part of the building. A factory foreman had a mostly glass office in the actual factory. Mrs. Blaylock made it clear, though, that Opal was to be directed first by herself and then by the other two secretaries as she might be assigned. Opal wasn't to bother any of the bosses.

Everything was more different than she'd imagined. Even the three ladies were unlike the country women she knew. The secretaries looked like women Opal had seen in shops in Vicksburg. They wore high heels, stockings, pretty skirts and blouses or shirtwaist dresses with petticoats. They wore earrings and maybe a bracelet or necklace. Some of her teachers had dressed like this. Dressing nice made the ladies at work look pretty even when they weren't, like Mrs. Blaylock who frowned all the time and had an odd mole on her forehead. Maybe that's why she frowned.

Opal was sure that Momma had been pretty once, back before she married and life got hard. None of her first three children reached five years of age. One was stillborn; one had pneumonia; and one had polio. That sister had lived for a while after Opal was born, but not long enough for Opal to remember her. Momma did the remembering and the crying, too. Losing those little ones was probably why Momma held Opal so close to home. Being naturally shy and obedient, Opal never pushed the boundaries. Now she was a high school graduate adult with a job, and the boundaries were way off in the distance.

By the time Daddy retired a few weeks later, Opal had mostly learned her job even though the mimeo machine still challenged her.

One of her favorite tasks was taking correspondence and orders to Mr. Foster, the plant foreman. Entering the factory was nearly like materializing over the rainbow. There was almost a yellow brick road. Of course it was only two, wide yellow lines painted on the floor that marked off a safe walkway. No one from the front office except the big bosses was to step outside this path to Mr. Foster's glassed-in office. She never even let the toe of her shoe touch the lines.

The sounds and smells of the factory were magic: the whirring, clicking songs of the machines and the delicious aroma of leather and machine oil. It was sweet and primal. Opal always breathed deeply of the scent and smiled. Out there was where Daddy had worked so long on the machine that cut the soles of shoes to each size he was directed.

Back in the office, she'd made a friend. Miss Corliss was secretary to the sales manager. He got most of the mail so Opal had cause to be at Miss Corliss' desk at least once a day. Corliss was the youngest and prettiest of the secretaries, and she seemed very smart. She always had a smile for Opal and a few words of greeting.

When Opal had made a mess with the mimeo on some of Corliss' work, she had gone to the workroom with Opal and showed her how to avoid the mistake.

"Sweetie, don't scrunch up your pretty face to cry," Corliss had told her. "Everyone makes mistakes when learning something new." Corliss squeezed Opal's arm reassuringly. At that moment, Opal would have stuck her hand in fire if Corliss asked. Opal's parents were good people. They loved her and provided what she needed, but there was little conversation or demonstration of affection. They were plain folk occupied with life other than Opal. Corliss was different. She sparkled. She laughed. She looked so pretty and smelled so good. She was kind to Opal and gave her tips and advice on doing her work and pleasing Mrs. Blaylock. This pretty lady liked Opal, and it made Opal proud. She'd never had a friend like Corliss.

If there was no mail for the sales manager, Opal made up another reason to go to Corliss' desk. Sometimes Opal took a little package of cookies to Corliss when she and Momma baked over the weekend.

Mrs. Blaylock noted the time Opal spent at Corliss' desk and advised the girl to stick to business.

Mrs. Blaylock said, "This isn't a soda shop, young lady. You do your visiting somewhere else."

One day Corliss surprised Opal. "Sweetie, don't bring your lunch tomorrow. I'm going to fix a special lunch for you and me, and we'll eat in the workroom. No one can fuss at us on our lunch break."

Opal hadn't the courage to tell Momma not to make a lunch, so she hid hers behind some supplies in the workroom. Anyway, if Corliss didn't really mean it, Opal would still have the sack lunch from home. But promptly at noon, Corliss appeared in the workroom, brown eyes shining, and with a large paper bag. "Little girl, wait 'til you see the lunch I made."

On the work table Corliss laid out the feast: cold chicken sandwiches piled high with garden tomatoes, pickles, crisp lettuce and mayonnaise; mustard potato salad, and two slices of rhubarb pie. Corliss dug out plates, utensils and napkins. Her dark curls fell about her face as Opal watched, enchanted. Opal followed Corliss' lead and began eating when her friend settled to the meal. It was their secret party.

"Opal, dear, quit fidgeting with your dress and eat your lunch. Don't you like it?"

"Oh, yes ma'am, it's delicious. You've given me such a pleasure. I – I'm just embarrassed."

"Sweet girl, you've nothing to be embarrassed about. What's wrong?"

"I'm not good enough. Miss Corliss, you're so good to me, and I'm so . . . nothing. I'm ashamed of the way I look, the way I dress, being so plain, not so smart. You, Miss Thelma and Mrs. Blaylock, you're all something. And you look like something."

"Opal, I don't want to pry, but do you give all your paycheck to your parents?"

"Yes, ma'am. That's what I'm supposed to do."

"But your Daddy," continued Corliss, "he gets a pension from the factory. Surely they don't need all your check."

"I never questioned. Daddy's been feeling sickly lately and there are doctor bills. My little money is needed."

Corliss served up a slice of pie to Opal. "I just wonder. Surely you should pay something to your parents like I pay rent to my boarding house, but you should also keep a little something for yourself, too. Does your mother make your clothes?"

"Yes."

"And you'd like something different, wouldn't you? Here's what I think." Corliss reached across the work table and took Opal's hand. "You talk to your mother. You agree on an amount that she needs from your check and you put aside something for yourself. After a couple of weeks or so, I'll take you shopping to a place where you can buy some pretty clothes that aren't expensive and will make you feel good. Do you think you can do that?"

Miss Corliss squeezed her hand, and Opal knew she could follow that lead.

Momma was surprised to hear Opal's proposal, but she agreed after some discussion. Three weeks later, Corliss planned to pick up Opal and take her to the dress shop.

The car Corliss drove was old, but it was her own. She was independent. Opal had waited at the living room window since breakfast so she wouldn't keep her friend waiting when she arrived. Momma was impatient with Opal's fussiness. Finally the old car drove up to the porch and Corliss stepped out, more sparkling than ever in casual summer slacks and a crisp blouse. Opal met her on the front porch trying not to appear star-struck. Momma held back in the living room.

Corliss, lithe and bubbly, hopped up the wooden porch steps and gave Opal a kiss on the cheek. "We'll have such fun today," she gushed.

Opal took her inside to meet Momma. Daddy couldn't come out. He was very weak now. Momma greeted Corliss politely, but cautiously, and Opal hopped in the car to go to Vicksburg.

The dress shop was small. Corliss knew the sales clerks and the location of all the best bargains. She quickly found a suitable skirt, blouse and dress for Opal to try on. Since she'd always worn homemade clothes, the dress shop was foreign, forbidding to Opal.

"Not that one," said Opal. "I'm too plump for that one with so many ruffles. That's what Momma would say."

"You leave it to me." Corliss led Opal down a short hall and into a curtained cubicle. "Take your dress off, sweetie. I'll be right back."

In the privacy of the dressing room, Opal shed her homely dress and wondered if she should slide out of her slip. She crossed her arms across her chest instead.

Corliss appeared at the curtain, pushing it aside and laughing at Opal's blush.

"Oh, look at you, Miss Modesty. You must try these. I think they're really you, and they're marked down." Corliss had returned with a pastel, shirtwaist dress and a tan, flared skirt and middy blouse with military-type buttons.

Corliss handed Opal the blouse and studied Opal's young, rounded form from her neck to her toes. Under her friend's scrutiny, Opal fumbled with the small buttons.

"Here, let me help." Corliss' voice was husky now.

As instructed, Opal stood still, hands at her sides. Corliss stepped closer and reached for the first button. If Corliss had any reservations, she overcame them. Her head dropped to Opal's neck; her hands sought Opal's young breasts. Opal cried out and stepped back, bumping into the wall. The woman and girl stared at each other wordlessly.

On Monday morning, Opal stayed in bed. She told Momma that she didn't feel good and that she should stay home today and from now on to help tend to Daddy. So, home she stayed. There was no shame in that. No one ever questioned her decision.

When The Music's Over

Scott Howdeshell

Who conjured up those parking lot
fist fights where the gravel and dirt
found all the concavities of the spine
and nestled in there like homesteaders
lit on freedom, like bootleggers in
stifling hot August dreams?
Would to God it might rain
and let out some of this combustible
earnestness, slit it open like an
envelope fresh from Kansas City,
crisp twenties folded within the letter
full of misspelled bloodline fury.
I heard a street preacher with an
amplifier in the same parking lot
where a wrecker sported brush-painted flames
on the quarter panels; I reckoned
I was close to home.
Who boiled up this telluric mess,
this ride through low-lying fog
and limp power lines?

The Marsh

Scott Howdeshell

Sized up the barrel house
and drove straight through that
sumbitch, I like the taut murmur-line
where everyone is afraid of what's next.
Some fool in melted dreamer's clothes
carries a hatchet and pulls a swollen cigarette
out from underneath the mess of Bing cherries
in his rusted wheelbarrow.
Seven octoroon babies cried
when you left
and I wondered where the song was
in that.
Remember that family that got lost
in Coohatchie Marsh, I
found the father's fiddle,
catgut strings now more like chickenskin out the fryer
and it smelled louder than sex
louder than the sacred hem of her
broken dress.
I gave it back to the moon
and the moonshine
with all its lousy reckoning
'cause I don't welch on no
blissful bet.

The Great Depression
Scott Howdeshell

A happenstance of ugly bibles
and withered gladiolas
gathered in the floor
and she gave a wooden stare
towards yonder room
where a mess of children
painted their white bellies
with bacon grease and stabbed
their butter knives
aimlessly at a sly wasp.
Big Sandy pined on the radio,
warbling about a stack of bills
and momma's medicine
while that wasp made a beeline
for the front yard junker Dodge,
the low mudbrown buzz
a metronome for the Fly-Rite Boys'
sad reprise.
She bent to her knees saying,
"My spirit has done turned to molasses."

Daddy Issues

Dan Leach

We got a six-pack and I drove her out to the water tower on the edge of town. The sun had sunk, but in its absence the sky hadn't yet gone to night. It was still tattered rags of pink and chalky blue. It was still evening when we climbed that ladder, more clouds than stars, more light than darkness. The view from up there wasn't much—some fields, a couple roads, a yellow clapboard house. But when you're sixteen you can't be too picky about where you drink, especially if you're drinking with a preacher's daughter.

Drinking made me quiet. Not moody, I don't think, but close to it. After two, I got thoughtful and slightly fatigued, like that feeling of lying in bed not asleep but not quite awake either, slowly slipping, everything turning hazy and black and sweet, consciousness leaking out like water from a crack in a cup. That was me. I liked to drink and watch the fields and not think about anything much at all. I liked the sensation of emptiness.

When she drank, though, she got mouthy. Her voice took on a strained, high-pitched quality and every other thing was about her Dad, about what a hateful, hard man he was, about how this time next year she would be emancipated and living with her cousin two counties over. For her, drinking was like kicking in an anthill. And it only took one beer.

One beer would get her going and I would do my best to listen, tempted to drift off into the fields, but trying to focus, trying to understand all the things racing around inside of her.

It wasn't easy. My own father, who didn't set foot in a church except Christmas and Easter, was one of the more amiable guys I knew. It didn't matter that he worked ten hours at a job he hated, or that money was usually tight and my mother, open book that she was, did a horrible job hiding her anxieties. No, my father came through the door with a smile and he damn-sure found a way, night after night, to lift us up. My father made us feel loved. If he did nothing else, he did that—he found a way to make us feel loved.

"Do you know he used to make me act in the Hell House every year?" she said, finishing her first can and chucking it into the field below us.

"What's a Hell House?" I said, half-way knowing, but wanting to make sure anyway.

"You don't know what a Hell House is?" she said and cracked open a second beer.

I shook my head and shrugged. She let out a sigh and took a long sip. "Must be nice to have normal parents."

"Come on," I said, trying in my own way to keep the mood up. "My parents made me do plenty of stuff I hated."

"Like what?" she said.

"Like the week before Christmas, I remember, we always had to go door to door in our neighborhood and sing "Winter Wonderland" and all those other songs. I hated it. For one, none of us could sing. For two, half the people shut the door in our face like we were trying to sell them something. It was awful. Freezing too."

She gave me that look—the one that said "It's not the same"—and shook her head from side to side. I knew that look well for all the times she put it on me. I should say, though, that there was no condescension in it. There was no arrogance in her at all. Relative to the rest of our town, my upbringing was "normal," and this fact humbled her. It gave her a modesty that was, to me, unbearably appealing relative to most kids our age who spent all their energy trying to get approval or pity or validation for one thing or another. She was different. When she talked about a thing, she didn't want anything from you. She just wanted to talk. I wondered if that wasn't the home-schooling that did that.

"A Hell House," she said. "Is something Daddy's church did twice a year. They would take the sanctuary and cover everything in black sheets. The walls, the pulpit, everything in black. Make it look all creepy."

She paused, apparently wanting me to envision this. And I did, as far as such a thing was possible. But I had never been in her father's church. Truth is, if asked, I probably couldn't envision the churches I had been in.

"Then they take these lights," she said. "Red lights, meant to look like fire and coming out in the shapes of flames. And they shine them all over the black sheets to make it look like Hell. They do this twice a year and people, tons of them, come to the church and let Daddy lead them on a tour."

"A tour? Of what?"

"They act out these scenes."

"Scenes?" I said, when she paused so long it seemed she needed help finishing the thought.

"I don't want to talk about this," she said, eyes shut, inhaling through her nose and exhaling through her mouth like someone trying to catch their breath.

"Then don't," I said and lit up a cigarette. "Talk to me about something else. Talk to me about school. How's Greene's class?"

She laughed like I knew she would and for a minute the conversation seemed redeemed. I opened another beer, careful not to drink too fast, but eager to keep my buzz.

"Mrs. Greene is crazy," she said. "Did you hear what she did to Buddy Campbell?"

"You mean when she washed his mouth out with soap after he lied about having a dip in?"

"No," she said, laughing.

"You mean when she called him a dumb sum-bitch in front the class?"

"No," she said. "That was a couple weeks back. I'm talking about this past week."

I shook my head, glad to see her smiling.

"No, I hadn't heard then. What did Buddy do this time?"

"He was cheating on a test," she started. "The genius that he was, he had all the answers written on the bottom of his shoe."

I laughed, not only because I had seen Buddy pull stunts like that, but also because Mrs. Greene had caught me cheating last year and I still remembered the fire in her eyes and how when she got me alone, out in the hallway, she talked through her teeth in a tone that made my neck go prickly like a mutt's. "I hate cheaters and I hate liars," she said. Silly and sweet as she could be, Mrs. Greene had a wrath that wasn't anything to mess with. I never cheated again, not in her class at least. Some things you don't forget.

"So Buddy is about halfway through his test and Mrs. Greene sees him doing it. Plain as day, she sees him getting an answer off his shoe. Only, she was across the room, at her desk, when she noticed it. And you know Mrs. Greene, too smart to go charging straight at him. So she gets up and makes like she's fixing a bulletin board over by Buddy's desk. All casual and calm. Just pretending to fix her bulletin board and not suspecting anything. And Buddy, too dumb to put his foot down, just kept on taking his test, cheating right there in the open."

It occurred to me then that I had heard this story. I knew exactly how it ended. Still, though, I didn't say anything and decided to let her finish it. You can tell a lot about a person by the way they tell a story, by what they leave in and what they take out.

"So Mrs. Greene is over there with her bulletin board," she continued.

"And everyone's focusing on their test. This was a major test, right? Everyone's all stressed out and focused and worried they'll run out of time. Then, out of nowhere, there is this loud crashing sound and Buddy is screaming his head off. Everyone looks up to see what's going on and Mrs. Greene has Buddy by the ankle. I mean, actually grabbed him by the ankle."

To illustrate she tried to reach down and grab her own ankle, but stumbled badly and almost went crashing into the railing before I grabbed her.

"Easy," I said, trying to pull her up but instead pulling her into me.

The booze had loosened her up and she practically fell into my arms, her face burying itself in my chest, the hand not holding the can slipping around my waist and attaching itself to my hip before I knew what had happened. Suddenly we were holding each other. Her hair was right beneath my face, the smell of strawberries filling up my nose. Without thinking about it, I kissed the top of her head. She stayed where she was when I did that. The sky, I noticed, was more blue than pink now, the lowering tide of light disappearing behind the horizon.

Eventually she let go, grabbed another beer, and continued the story like nothing ever happened.

"So Buddy's trying to kick away, but Greene's got him good, trying to yank his shoe off, and screaming, 'I caught you, I caught you.' She kept tugging at it until the shoe came off.

Buddy, one shoe on, mumbled a few curse words and said something about her being crazy before hobbling out of the room. She took the shoe and locked it up in her desk drawer. Evidence, I guess. Anyway, we died laughing. Even when Greene threatened detentions, we couldn't stop. I don't think anybody finished that test. How could we?"

"Aren't you glad you came to public school?" I said and as soon as it came out, I realized my mistake.

We drank for a while in silence after that. A pick-up came tearing down one the roads. I watched it, figuring it was heading for the house. But it just kept on driving, a pair of tail-lights on its way to nowhere. I kept thinking about strawberries and the way her body felt pressed against mine.

"Yeah, well at least I'm learning something," she eventually said. "Mrs. Greene might be crazy, but at least she teaches. Daddy called himself a teacher but all he was was an assigner."

"So that's why you're so independent," I said, keen to keep the talk positive.

Illustration by Stephen Smith

"Right," she said and rolled her eyes. "I remember when I was in fifth grade, I asked him about something in the science book. It was something about dinosaurs and I didn't understand it. He was in his chair, like always, and asked me to read it to him. I did. I wish I could remember what it was. It would have been something about the Triassic and Jurassic periods, something about the earth being millions of years old."

"Good memory," I said.

But she shook her head and said, "Let me finish the story and you'll see why."

"Okay."

"See, Daddy didn't believe in dinosaurs."

"What do you mean?"

"I mean he didn't believe in them. He denied their existence."

"Hold on, though. Aren't there are fossils and stuff? Actual proof."

"Sure."

"And he knows about that?"

"Sure."

"How can you know about that stuff and not believe?"

"He said fossils were a fabrication invented by liberals to spread evolution."

"So what did he do to the science book?"

"He charged across the room, snatched it out of my hand, and threw it in the fire. Called it 'secular trash' and spit into the flames," she said.

"You're joking."

"I'm not," she said. "He had all kinds of crazy beliefs."

"Like what."

"You really want to know?"

"I asked, didn't I?"

Once she got going, she went on for a while, talking about everything from the President being the anti-Christ to AIDs being a curse God put on homosexuals. I listened, laughing when she did, but otherwise staying quiet. It was a difficult thing for me to grasp. The few times I met her father, he seemed intense, but by no means insane. I thought of him as I thought of most the preachers I had met—different from my own dad, but decent to the degree that they served a decent God. I thought all preachers served a decent God. To learn that I was dead-wrong was a bit disorienting. "How," I thought but did not say, "Can someone who believes in God believe in such hateful things?" Half the time she was talking, I was trying to reconcile this in my mind.

The other half of the time I couldn't help but think of my Dad. What were his beliefs?

College football and John Wayne movies? A steak served rare and cold can of Coors? I knew he loved Christmas and watched documentaries on the Civil War. Once I heard him get upset about a friend of his who couldn't find a job. But I had never heard my Dad talk about "beliefs." My dad made jokes. He told stories. I don't how he felt about liberals or, for that matter, dinosaurs. I wondered what he and Aimee's father would talk about if they sat down together. I wondered what my Dad would do in a Hell House. Then I wondered if two people could both be right at the same time.

I guess she could tell that I was drifting because she stopped.

"Crazy, right?" she said, almost embarrassed.

"Yeah," I said, and to lessen her embarrassment, I shared some stories about my Uncle Jimmy. He was my mother's younger brother. She called him a "character" amongst other things. Uncle Jimmy had his fair share of conspiracy theories and was a pretty nasty racist to boot. I told her about the time he built a bunker in his backyard and filled it with can goods and semi-automatic weapons. I told her what he called people who weren't white and then told her about the time Uncle Jimmy started a fight with a Hispanic crossing guard and had to be rushed to the hospital for two cracked ribs and a broken jaw. I figured that might tip the scales and make her a little more comfortable. I knew it worked when she started smiling again and said, "The world's full of crazies, ain't it?"

"Sure is," I said.

"Maybe you're one of them," she said and while I was thinking of something clever to say kissed me on the mouth.

It was a clean kiss, quick and singular, and she backed away as soon as it was finished. For a moment, we just stared at one another. Then I stepped forward and took her face in my hands. It felt small and fragile somehow and I just held it for a moment, not caring how it seemed. She closed her eyes, parted her lips, and started leaning in. And because I didn't want to make her feel uncomfortable, I kissed her, even though that's not what I wanted to do. Weird as it sounds, weird as it was: I wanted to hold her face and just look at it. I wanted to hold her face until I had memorized every part of it. The freckles on her nose, the tiny scar above her eye, the greens and browns inside her eyes, and every last hair on her head: I wanted to know it all.

Instead, though, I kissed her, afterwards letting my lips trace the distance from her lips to her ear, where I whispered, "You're beautiful. You are nothing less than beautiful." Her cheek against mine, I felt her smile. Then she found my ear and whispered something back, only, just she said it, though, a strong wind came through, making the inside of my ear roar like a conch. Before I could ask what she said, our lips were together again, our hands, light as feathers, floating from one place to another. I was still wondering what she said when I put my hand beneath her shirt. It sounded like "Take me"? Was that it? Was it "Take me"? Or was it "Save me"? I could not, for the life of me, stop to ask her which.

Maybe it was the beer or the way the light was falling, but after we started kissing, one movement bled into another until we found ourselves in my backseat, two sets of sweaty limbs tangled desperate and ungracious but somehow melded together, somehow working together to get a place we had never been.

Back of my car, the blood red sun spilling in through the windshield: we made it. Her first, my first.

And after it was done, we lied on our backs and said nothing and listened to each other breathe as the last of the light faded from the sky. I wanted to prop myself up on an elbow and look into her face, to see if it was the same face I had held up on the water tower, or if something had changed. I couldn't have explained why, but I felt like something had changed, that her face wasn't the same face and my eyes weren't the same eyes. Lying there in the backseat, I felt like we had stepped into something new, crossed an invisible border or something, and now that we were there, there was no going back. There was no going back to who we used to be.

I must have fallen asleep because when I opened my eyes, she was sitting up and saying something.

"What?" I said, propping myself up on my elbow and trying to figure out how long I was out.

"Do you have a lighter?" she said.

"In the thing," I said, pointing to the change compartment.

She grabbed the lighter and snapped out a flame.

"You want a cigarette?" I asked.

"No," she said and continued staring into the flame.

I watched her watch the light, tiny golden discs floating on top of her irises, her mouth hanging open like a slot. Something was happening to her face. It started in her eyes and spread down to her mouth and, in less than a second, I felt like I was looking at a stranger.

"The lights would be off when the people first came into the Hell House," she said, eyes fixed on the flame, that horrible look consuming her features.

"And Daddy would meet them in the lobby with nothing more than a lighter."

I wanted to say something. I opened my mouth. There was nothing, no words for me to say.

"And with all those people watching he would take the flame and bring right up to his hand."

About the time I noticed that she had positioned her other hand over the lighter, she clicked the wheel to ignite a new flame and lowered that hand on top of it, letting out a choked whimper as it singed the center of her palm. Paralyzed, I watched her white skin retreat, the flesh peeling back like flower petals. I watched her burning. At first her arm jerked back, but, as if some invisible weight was attached to it, she lowered it again, causing the flame to tear deeper and release a rancid scent into the car. The entire gesture, from the click of the wheel to me knocking the lighter loose, could not have lasted more than a second.

"Are you crazy?" I said.

She was crying and her hand was trembling badly but she extended it in my direction, practically pushing the bloody patch into my face. I grabbed her by the wrist, but still she thrust that hand towards my eyes. I remember how it looked. I remember how it smelled.

"This," she said, ripping free from my grip but still extending it outwards. "This is what he would do in front of those people in the lobby. Right before opening the doors to the sanctuary, he would burn his hand so they could see it. Then, he would open the doors to the Hell House and say, 'Now imagine eternity. Imagine burning for all of eternity.'"

Something had happened without my noticing it. I suddenly wanted nothing more than to go back in time and still be up there drinking beer on the water tower. I wished I could go back even further, before I ever brought her out here.

"That's what a Hell House is," she said.

Knowing that there was no going back, that, here and now, she was talking about her Daddy because, in a way, she needed to, I decided to go along. I laid a hand on her shoulder and said, "Is that really what he believes?"

"Yes."

"That everybody is going to Hell?"

"Not everybody."

"Just the bad people?"

"Not exactly," she said and looked as if she meant to say more, but then stopped. "Close enough though."

"Is that what you believe?"

"I don't know what I believe."

"Did you?" I asked. "At one time, I mean."

"Yes."

"What changed?"

"I don't know," she said. "Maybe nothing."

"Let me see your hand," I said and extended mine.

She didn't question this, just laid hers, knuckle-down, into mine.

The wound shone in what was left of the evening's light.

"That's pretty bad," I said, not knowing the first thing about how to treat a burn.

"Imagine eternity," she said and coughed into her good hand.

"Come on," I said, opened the door, and led her out into the night.

Later, after we had gone to Walgreen's and a pharmacist had fixed her up, after we had said goodbye and I had dropped her off at her friend's house, after everything was over and it was just me driving through town, I tried to take the road that led back to my house.

I thought about my parents and how both of them would still be up, sprawled out on the couch, watching television. I would come in and they would call me. They would tell me to sit down and ask about my night. And I could tell them everything or I could tell them nothing, and that wouldn't change how they looked at me. They loved me, seemingly without condition.

I came up on another road that would take me to that house, but my hand on the wheel didn't budge. I kept on driving, pushing further out towards roads I had never seen, towards the darkened fields on the edge of town. I wanted to turn around. I tried to, but was not able. I felt the cool leather of the steering wheel against the tender center of my palm and I couldn't, for the life of me, stop thinking about eternity, how it had already begun.

December 1976
Robert Lee Kendrick

In the kitchen lights' yellowing sheen,
my mother's slow breath
curls butter smoke over a skillet.
Blue gas licks the silence.

She's breathed sugar
for nine hours at Beich, machine-molding
chocolate hearts,
& the egg in her palm sours her stomach.

Night smudges its face
on the window & coughs. Teeth fall
from the rain gutter
as I glue together the skeleton

of a toy plane that won't fly.
Her cigarette ash
stretches & breaks on a saucer
as she shuts her eyes.

The brittle shell
shatters on iron. A white bird
flutters & dies.

Waiting Out the Wind

Richard Weaver

Three weeks alone
before a skiff of fishermen beached
to untangle their handlines,
asking me, was I lonely?

And what was I doing here?
I told them
I was drawing birds
and hadn't been lonely yet.

Satisfied, they left, leaving me
a small redfish to complement
my breakfast of raisins and beans.
Until that time,

the island had been mine alone.
I'd caught oysters in the mudflats,
and drawn some days
until my eyes would no longer see.

I found shells for Mere to string,
putting them in my hat for safekeeping.
Sometimes I swam in the waves,
delighting in the patterns spilling

out of the churned foam. Or I'd walk out
until my feet could just touch bottom,
the daymoon dancing with me.
Tomorrow with the wind
southeast at my back,
I'll sail toward the Biloxi lighthouse, and home.

But today the bitterns call my name,
and the catbirds make a game
of hide-and-seek along the shore reeds.
Even the gallinules have come out
to ask me to stay.

Rabbit Springs

Richard Weaver

Possums, raccoon, kildeer, loons,
grackles, peeps, dogris, sculpin.
If they're afraid it's not of me.

We gather at the spring
to drink from the flowing well.
On clear nights the beach glows

with light from the Biloxi shore
and we bask together in its otherworldness.
But mostly the world is only this island.

And gnats! Always gnats and mosquitoes.
My blood flies across the gulf
in their swollen bodies. I fill

my jugs and rinse the day's
hard-earned salt from my hat.
My face glows with the moon's life.

I'm alone. I watch the tide wash in
and walk the dark sand toward home,
one star a thousand full moons.

The Swimmer

Richard Weaver

Each moment turning in my hand
your oak body reveals
its simple desire
to return as water.
Though I found you
not far from my cottage
where you had fallen during a storm,
I could feel beneath the bark I stripped
a perfect form, an energy,
a life beyond my working hands.
I turn you now
away from the angling sun
toward the beach and the waiting waves
where Sissy and I swim each day.
An axe and an adze are all I need
before you rise, naked
from a pool of shavings. And risen
into light, patient and sleek in shadow,
look to the sea if you must.
Look there until I return
bearing the island's gifts:
star coral, squamosa, morning cowrie.
They will be ours
until we are the sea's again.

Windbound

Richard Weaver

Even with the morning star watching over me
and the red-winged blackbird singing
my praises to all who would listen,
the wind has headed me, determined this morning
to last me out. I land, set up camp on Ship Island,
and watch the clouds clustering in tight knots.
Muted, almost colorless,
I can only accept
this decision as penance, and wait
for the judgment to pass.
Or turn like the tide upon itself.

Voyage Home
Richard Weaver

I look out a window
overlooking the Mississippi
in the city where I was born,
in the city where I am dying.
Sissy sings a good song nearby
but a man in my position hears
too many things and knows only one.
Outside, the river is a ring
with no beginning. Two pigeons
are making a nest on the Canal Street ferry.
They dance, circling each other
to an old song. The male
fluffs himself up proudly,
Sure of their love. They kiss.
When he flies away for string or straw
she turns back to the nest,
her instinct an anxious song filling the air.
Too soon the ferry will sound its bell
and move to the river's other side.
Too soon he will return with his straw.
Soon the river of our honeymoon
will flow on without me.

Pachelbel Braids His Daughter's Hair

Heidi Espenscheid Nibbelink

I.

In another place, in another time, the musician leans his head against the wall, closes his eyes. A cigarette smolders, abandoned in a saucer. He feels his heartbeat throb where his head touches the bricks, plodding, soulless. His soul resides on the other side of the wall, beating against the bricks with useless wings.

"Papa?" An Anna comes to him. Roseanna. Always, now, it will be Roseanna. Her hands are full: combs, hair brush, ribbons.

She turns, wedging herself between his knees, facing the window. He takes the brush and begins to work, starting at the bottom, combing the ends as he has watched his wife do a hundred times, working his way higher up the waterfall of tangles cascading down Roseanna's back. There is a troublesome knot, he switches to the comb, tugging, teasing apart. The girl flinches.

"Am I hurting you?"

"It's all right," she says. Her elbows rest on his knees. She keeps her gaze fixed through the glass, across the road where the rocks churn the brook to froth, where an osprey perches on a deadfall, attuning one eye to slight motions below.

She is being brave, and he is grateful. He pauses to take a drag on his cigarette, then separates the girl's hair into strands, crossing and weaving as his wife has taught him, his fingers less clever than hers but sure enough. He ties the end of the braid with a bit of green ribbon.

"Turn around," he tells the girl. She turns, her mother's grey eyes regarding him steadily. He slides a silver comb above the left ear, then the right.

Roseanna pats her head, fingers the combs, tugs the end of her braid around to the front to inspect the ribbon tie. "Do I look the same?" she asks him. "Do I look the same as ever?"

"The same as ever," he assures her. It is the world around them that is changed, but of this there is no need to speak. "Now go," he tells her. "Tante Greta will see you to school."

The solid heels of her leather boots echo across the wooden floor. The last glimpse he has of her is the bright green of her hair-ribbon, a hopeful blemish against her somber-colored dress. He reaches again for his cigarette, but it has gone out. He leans his head against the bricks, searching for strength to gather.

II.

In another place, in another time, "Such beautiful boots," are the first words the musician says to Anna. She has forgotten herself on the river-bank in the late afternoon sunshine. While her mother went into the shops, Anna took off her hat and stretched herself on the grass. She closed her eyes, delighting in the warmth of the sunlight on her face, the breeze playing with her curls. Anna snaps her eyes open and looks down at herself, realizes the man can see a great deal more of her legs than just her boots. She pulls herself up to the most dignified sitting position she can manage and says, "Pardon me?"

"Your boots are magnificent, forgive me for noticing." His voice is low and warm, but she has trouble making out his expression—the sun behind him halos his head in light, making her squint and shade her eyes. He holds out a hand and unthinkingly she accepts. He pulls her to her feet and now she can see the brown eyes and curls that match the honey-warm tones of his voice, which she will soon learn echoes the tone of the violin whose case he carries. "I am a man who notices beautiful things," he tells her. She hears her mother's voice calling her name from across the road.

III.

In another place, in another time Roseanna and Susanna have crept away from their mother who drowses in the sun with a book dropped against her chest, and play near the water's edge. They have been warned each day since they learned to toddle not to go to the river alone, but the fun of dropping sticks from one footbridge then racing downstream to the next footbridge to see which twin's stick made the journey fastest is too great for clever girls to resist. Roseanna's knees are skinned and muddy from her fall during the second race. Susanna has lost a boot lace among the reeds.

They are leaning over the rail of the downstream bridge, the limestone rough against their forearms as they pull themselves up on tiptoes, straining to see the bobbing noses of their racing sticks, when a heavy paw descends upon their narrow shoulders. "Girls!" Their gentle father is fierce in his black greatcoat, too warm for the day, with his omnipresent violin case slung over his shoulder. He drags them back to the house, roughly shoves them into their sleeping room. The lock clicks shut. The girls kneel before the window and crack open the shutter. They hear raised voices, the unmistakable smack of flesh on flesh, the sound of doors slamming. There is no dinner that night. In the grey and cloudy morning, father unlocks their door and calls them to breakfast. Their mother stays behind her closed bedroom door, leaving a seat empty at the table. Susanna opens her mouth to ask, but Roseanna kicks her under the table with a pointed boot toe.

IV.

In another place, in another time, Ghostanna folds herself in half, taking her head from the clouds, where she has been watching the tops of the thunderheads stack themselves into rounded towers of boulders, into slender spires of rose-colored minarets threaded with afternoon sunlight invisible to those below. She folds herself down through sunlight, through a floor of grey clouds, until she can peek her eye through the candle-lit window of her sister's room in the house where they once lived together, where she once died. She sees Roseanna kneel on the braided rug next to her bed, her lips moving in prayer. When she focuses, Ghostanna can summon a charge of energy through her elongated wisp of a being, a current pure enough to discharge a tiny spark from the end of her littlest finger.

"Give me a sign," Roseanna prays, and Ghostanna sparks a puff of wind strong enough to knock the bottle of toilet water from the edge of the dressing table.

Roseanna jumps. Ghostanna doesn't see her tears, the minutes spent picking up shattered glass, the gash on Roseanna's heel that opens when she steps on a shard, the crimson footprints left on the floorboards when Roseanna goes in search of a towel. Ghostanna is already straightening, lifting, letting the storm-front waft her upwards and westwards, where she will join the Gulf Stream and sail across the sea, where she will be a cloud-castle forming and reforming.

V.

In another place, in another time, the musician is her husband, and they cannot pay the rent. The landlady scowls at Anna each time she sees her, Anna looks down and walks past her quickly, noticing her own scuffed boots, her fraying hem. They cannot afford new things. In the closet at her father's house are rows of shoes—slippers for dancing, boots for riding, boots for rainstorms, boots for winter snows. Anna finds excuses not to leave the house, leaves the curtains drawn against the landlady's ire. Her husband notices her haunted mood. "What is the matter, my Anna? Why are you my Cloudy-Anna? Where is my Sunny-Anna?"

"Do not tease me, Johann. It is unkind."

"Cloudy-Anna, Cloudy-Anna," he sings, waltzing her into his arms and around their small room, falling down with her on the bed in the corner. Now leaving the windows covered seems like foresight.

VI.

In another place, in another time, Roseanna learns to walk again after the amputation. The wooden leg and foot attach with a complicated array of straps and buckles. Her father makes it his mission to find ever-softer pieces of padding. Instead of practicing his violin, he spends his evenings pouring over anatomical charts in huge volumes he borrows from the Bishop. He is searching for the perfect arrangement, contours that will seem as inevitable as nature. Eventually, Roseanna tells him to stop. "Let it be," she says. "Let me learn to be." In a few weeks, limping home from an evening walk along the river road, she hears a trill of arpeggios from the cottage window, then the sound of a melody, rising.

VII.

In another place, in another time, Cloudanna takes her violin from its case. She rosins the bow, tests the D-string. She summons up the music, rests the instrument in the welcoming notch of her shoulder, feels the familiar ache in her wrist as she positions the bow. She pauses, hovering just above the strings. "Start play," she says, and the track begins, filling the viewing lounge with music magnificent enough to accompany the stars rushing past the window. She plays, adding her single line to swell the cacophony.

Each of the crew has been allowed one comfort. Cloudanna brought her violin, Helvetica her two cats. For weeks Bartree dithered between the hand-printed works of Velmiginous Kalmath, which seemed the more erudite choice, or his set of obsidian-handled chef's knives, an anniversary gift from his lost partner Kelvina. "Don't worry about how it looks to others," Cloudanna told him, T-minus five days before their launch. "Bring the thing that makes you feel most like you." In the end, he chose the knives. Helvetica snorts when she unpacks them. "Cooking knives on a spaceship, Bartree? Really? It's not like you'll have anything to use them on."

"I don't care," Bartree says. "That's not what it's about."

"What is it about then?"

Bartree doesn't answer. He stacks the knife box on top of his equipment case and heads down the corridor.

"I'd better not see them out of your quarters," Helvetica calls after him. "There's a lot of delicate equipment about. Knives are dangerous." She outranks them both, and reminds them whenever it suits her. Cloudanna follows Bartree, and Helvetica is left alone, kneeling in the empty hallway.

VIII.

In another place, in another time, the musician wipes down his violin with a soft cloth.

He stows the instrument in its case, prepares to leave the empty cathedral. It is small, a minor building in a minor parish, but still he upholds his standards, staying after the other musicians have departed to practice the difficult passages, the familiar scales, the tricky arpeggios. The cottage he shares with his wife and twin babies is too small for serious practice. The family enjoys a fiddle tune or two, but home is no place for serious work. This time to him is precious, casting his sound down the nave where it bounces off the stone wall and returns to him, playing until the sweat soaks his back and dampens his curls, playing for no one but himself and the stained glass saints looking down from their windows.

Outside, his boots crunch on hard-packed snow. He wonders which Anna he will find at

home tonight—Sunny Anna, welcoming him with a mug of hot wine when he opens the cottage door with a gust of cold air, or Cloudy Anna, speaking in clipped sentences, cleaning the table too fiercely, not meeting his eyes. He has stayed too late, the little girls will be asleep. He will go into their room and caress their hair, plant a small kiss on each dreaming forehead. His feet move him from the village to home, his mind turns from domestic cares to solving the intonation problems in movement three. Minor cathedrals in minor parishes often have minor players. He will cut the ranks to one on a part for the opening sixteen measures. Is that delicate enough? Or will the wealthy second-chair violist complain to the Bishop, causing Johann to lose his appointment and driving his family further into want? He turns his collar against the cold, in the moonlight his labored breaths become fleeting white clouds.

IX.

In another place, another time, the Annas have returned to the foot bridge over the river. Each morning they breakfast with father before they walk down the road and part at the bridge, the girls with their school books, father with his violin case slung across his back. Each evening he returns as the stars emerge. He makes the evening meal jolly, teasing, calling for them to bring him more wine, more bread. He unpacks his violin and sets them dancing, playing faster and faster until red-faced and laughing they collapse on the floor at his feet.

Father has become larger, and mother smaller. She keeps to her room, rarely making an appearance at the table or in the yard. After breakfast the girls peek through her door to see if she's in the chair near the window or still abed. On rainy days she lets them climb into bed with her, where they smell her familiar sour smell, feel the lightness of her fingers as she brushes and braids their hair. After a time, the housekeeper comes to shoo them out. "Let her rest," the housekeeper says. "Why does she need so much rest?" Susanna asks. Under the quilt, mother turns her face to the wall. Every day becomes like the day before.

X.

In another place, another time, Cloudanna is assigned to D-Deck Engineering Support and Tactical Systems Maintenance. She spends her days testing and calibrating. There are brief moments of system failure and panic, but the auto backups always take over until she is able to effect repairs. Redundancy is her stalwart companion.

They have not had to use tactical systems yet, but Cloudanna keeps them in working order, the aft cannons and the fore laser-blasters. They are passing through a lightly travelled region. It has been well mapped, but reports of encounter are hard to come by. They are gathering data EmergiCorps will use to site the third engineered planetary cluster in their Utopia Project – the one they're naming Utopia Harmonia.

She and Bartree often cross paths in the dining area and eat their rations together. It is Bartree's first mission and he is anxious. She catches him pacing outside her work area sometimes, wearing a path in the faux-homey carpeting that makes her wonder if the whole ship is constructed of questionable material. One day she found a small paring knife outside her living quarters door. Bartree likes to quiz her on her ancestry. He's learned her four-times-great-grandfather was a composer.

"When did you realize it was music that made you feel most like you?"

"I don't remember. There was always music."

Bartree takes a sip of his water, keeping his eyes on her over the rim of his glass. His Adam's apple bobs violently as he drinks.

"Cloud Anna. Cloudanna," he says, as though searching for something he's misplaced. "That's an unusual name."

"Is it? I went to school with a RainEva."

"It's such a beautiful name, I mean."

CloudAnna studies the tips of her EmeriCorps-issued boots. She wonders how much time she has before she must notify Helvetica.

XI.

In the same place, in the same time, is it a joke or part of a grand design that an attack saves Cloudanna from the confrontation she was dreading? What's a sprinkle of laser-cannon fire from an unknown hostile compared to unpleasant personnel matters? They are manning the battle stations. They are executing evasive maneuvers. They sustain a direct hit on the living quarters and Cloudanna watches Bartree's knives, freed of their case, take a leisurely spin past the starboard window, as though a choreographed knife-ballet had been planned just for her. Another direct hit, this one nearer her position, and Cloudanna hears Helvetica commanding in her earpiece, "Fire at will! Fire at will!" Cloudanna presses the button on the sequence she programmed days earlier. She sees another flash. The cannons in D-Deck begin their synchronized blast patterns, lighting the void with a predictable steadiness, enhanced by a filigree of rapid fire from the fore-lasers. Their vehicle hurtles closer to the future site of Utopia Harmonia, but Cloudanna has already left the scene, stretching, elongating, reaching her wispy being away from the nearest star's weak gravity toward the Milky Way beyond.

Amplification
David Tuvell

Elvis took a MapQuest route
through Memphis, kept his doors
locked, windows up, down back
streets to the station.

He figured Prometheus for a liar,
so he hooked amps up to a turtle shell,
signed with Sun Studios,
soldiered with the Colonel under its heat lamp
to popcorn Apollo's royalties.

He girded his loins with gospel
music, carried the sword of righteous
dudes, rocked high and swung low,
causing a Great Schism in the sun's
chariot, then filled the cracks with packaging.

Elvis struck a rock for water, said:
I got places to be, come ye
to Woodstock, form a chain
and dissolve your livers.

In the Dark Field
David Brendan Hopes

Arthur liked to do boring things, but he was not a boring person, and that interested me. Back where I grew up we assumed that if it wasn't fun right off, it was not worth worrying about. Try the rutabaga once and then get on with your life. Go to the opera, hate it, never go back. Arthur was the type who'd go back ten times to see what people were raving about, then one day his face would light up and he'd get it, and become in turn one of THOSE people, yapping about great tenors and divas and La Scala and what have you. He had lots of friends, of a certain kind, and I wondered why he kept after me, until the thought crossed my mind that he was maybe treating me the same way, trying to cure an initial aversion by frequent and determined contact.

Arthur was absolutely non-discriminating when it came to information. He'd listen while the janitor told him, as though anybody had asked, how to choose the best mop for such-and-such a floor. He'd listen while my dumbass freshman roommate, Ricky or Dicky or whatever it was, went on about his dad and him were going to shoot tin cans off the fence all Thanksgiving break. I watched him listening to the waitress at the Moose Head Diner like she was Mrs. Shakespeare, and I was divided equally between the urge to mock and the urge to remake myself in his image, to empty the smarmy little vessel of my mind and let the rest of the world pour in. It was a passing fancy, but a strong one. We were in college, and surely that's what we all were supposed to be doing, asking questions, probing, inquiring. Most of my friends spent at least some of their energy trying to fend off information that was too unlike what they knew before. Not old Arthur. He could sit down in any room, amid any crowd, and come away with something learned, some new amazement about the multiplicity of the world. I wondered if he was Frankenstein's monster or somebody like, totally empty before he stepped onto campus.

Anyway, near the end of fall semester, Arthur conceived in his complicated heart the notion of going to Dollywood. Dollywood is an amusement park in Pigeon Forge, Tennessee, which started out as a bunch of other things–a Coal Mining theme park, a Famous Serial Killers of the Smokies theme park, I forget what all—but ended up as a kind of hillbilly heaven with Country singer Dolly Parton as patron saint. I had been there and he had not. Mom and dad took my sisters and me there long ago, and I retained a set of intense memories—the taste of vomit in your mouth after the coaster rides, which only cotton candy could take away, for instance—which I wanted to test against my present sensual armament. Arthur didn't seem the Dolly-wood type, if I remembered the place correctly, but he was the try-out-new-things type. I thought I should warn him about what he was in for, but when the moment came I realized I didn't know what he was in for. A ten year old sees one thing, a twenty-one year old another. Maybe he would be able to tell me what it was all about.

"Man, why do you want to go to Dollywood?"

"I've never been there. I keep hearing about it," Arthur said, lifting one blond eyebrow the way he does. You keep hearing about hell, too, but I doubt you want to go there. Still, I was game. Maybe I liked it when I was a kid. There'd been a few too many reefers between then and now for me to remember exactly.

Arthur had to drive because my tires were shot. I thought I mentioned that we should bring a buddy or two along to share the experience and the expense, but maybe I forgot, because his car was empty when he pulled up to my apartment and my buddies, Jo-Jo and Carnage and Alamo began to pile in the back seat. I had to ride shotgun because I'd hurt my knee in intramural soccer and it still hurt some if I didn't have room to stretch it out from time to time.

Arthur took Jo-Jo and Carnage and Alamo in stride, and they he, once they got over his rule about no smoking in the car. Alamo can be a card when he's in the mood, and he kept Arthur laughing most of the way. I was glad that the friends I have from two different segments of my life were getting along. I was glad also that Arthur was playing some pretty cool CDs, indie rock and the like, for it's a rule that the driver owns the airwaves and if the driver likes listening to crap, you're in for hours of misery. Alamo and Arthur got into a pretty detailed discussion about the Smiths, reciting lyrics to each other in a way which I found to be, after a while, alarming. While they quoted and cross-referenced, I watched the landscape rolling by, the blue mountains in the distance, the frost-browned grass on the sides of the road stretching up to the block walls of the outlet malls. The going was slow because of the thousands of shoppers crowding to the outlets in Sevierville and Pigeon Forge, it being the week before Thanksgiving and America's Christmas acqui-sition panic fully upon them. Arthur asked if we wanted to stop, and maybe one of us did, but he wouldn't have said so. I figured I could pick mom and my sisters up a few cute things in Dollywood, with the name written on it and all. They would appreciate that.

I don't think he knew what the lines of cars were after. "Look at all the traffic. Out here in the country and all. Is there a. . . I don't know. An attraction?" Arthur asked.

"All them outlets," said Carnage, waving his hand from the back seat toward the horizon.

"Outlets?"

"Yeah," Alamo continued, "where you get things cheap. You know, goods from all the big stores. They sell them cheap here."

Arthur considered this for a moment. "How cheap? What would I save if I went into that Eddie Bauer store and bought a coat?"

"You need a coat?"

"No. Just for instance."

"Couple of bucks."

"There are license plates from Florida, Alabama, Pennsylvania. . . ."

"Yeah, so? My mom comes here from Atlanta every year."

"But you can't save enough to make up for gas and traveling time and all that."

Carnage was a sort of Sociology major at the time, so he chimed in, "It's the swarm mentality, you know? You like to be with hundreds of other people doing the same thing they are doing because you have the idea that it must be the right thing if everybody is doing it. Christmas morning, after all the gifts are unwrapped, you can brag about the forty bucks you saved by going to the outlet stores. Nobody mentions the two hundred that went into gas and lunch and—if you're from freaking Michigan the way that lady is— motel rooms. Everybody knows it, but it's not mentioned."

Jo-Jo chimed in from the left rear window, "It's just like organized religion."

Everything nasty or questionable was like organized religion to Jo-Jo, who was a self-begotten Native American Buddhist, but I could see Arthur didn't know this was an automatic response, and was really considering it. All he said, though, all he said from the point to the Dollywood parking lot was, "Hmmmm."

You take a tram car from the parking lot to the gates of the amusement park, and while we were waiting and riding, Arthur had time to complete his survey of his new companions. He was really pretty good at that, asking a few precise questions, showing real interest, filing it all away under the thatch of blond hair. Turned out both Alamo and Carnage were poets. They never told me. They'd told Arthur as we were stomping around against the cold, waiting for the next tram, smooth as if it had been their phone numbers. Arthur asked to read their poetry, and I bet the two of them no more than got home that night than they were e-mailing Arthur the hip-hop secrets of the hearts.

Jo-Jo had nothing to share poetry-wise. Jo-Jo was tactile. He felt his way through the world, pressing his skinny body against things he wanted to understand. I watched him press up against Arthur as we walked. Arthur moved aside the first couple of times, until he realized the touch was a gesture and not an accident. Then he went on as though Jo-Jo were not walking beside him, close as a shadow, as though Jo-Jo had not taken him by the hand as an apprehensive child his father's in a place of confusion.

We all bunched up at the gate and paid our money, and as we gathered on the other side, this lady snapped our photo. What a gaggle of misfits! Autumn chill hid some of our individuality under overcoats, but there was Alamo's inevitable dirt blue ski-cap (evident summer, winter, bed, shower— though he didn't shower that often); there were Carnage's ripped-to-shreds, true-to-his-name army surplus khakis hung with military memorabilia; there was Jo-Jo with one big flannel shirt flapping around his fencepost body, as though the bones and skin that made up most of him didn't feel the cold. And there were Arthur and I, looking pretty normal, I thought, though Arthur had worn a bright red shirt and I was so extraordinarily handsome that it did rather jar the eye.

I'd worried about who would dominate the crew (I meant to, if it came to that) but the surprise and wonder of the place was so great that we just naturally wandered around in a clump, babes-in-the-woods style, taking it all in together. It provided a form of protection, I guess, as well as a portable chorus for our observations. One theme pervaded. As Jo-Jo remarked, "They're all dressed like Mee-Maw's Mee-Maw." Most of the employees were, in fact, got up as old-time mountain people in bonnets and buckskins. There were coonskin caps and bolts of gingham and jugs with three x's on them, which were meant to allude to moonshine. But it was Christmas, too, so there was an intermingling Victorian theme: top hats and big elaborate dresses, and one tall gent going around muttering, "Bah, humbug!"

Arthur said, "They're not missing a trick, are they?"

It was true that somebody had made sure that whatever memory you had of Christmas, whatever rumor came to you from the Christmases of your grandmothers back in the coves under the mountains, whatever echoes remained from a production of The Christmas Carol you played Bob Cratchit in during middle school, it was represented in the shops and walkways of Dollywood, hung with lights and ablaze with tinsel. Arthur in particular seemed awestruck. "There's no principle of selection," he said. "It's like . . . you know what it's like?"

"No," Carnage responded, really interested, "What's it like?"

"It's like if some big disaster came upon us, a release of toxic gas or all the volcanoes in the world exploding at once, and we were pretty much wiped out, every man, woman and child on the earth gone, except it was Christmas, you know, Christmas Eve, and a few malls were left standing out in the boondocks, a few malls out in Nebraska or Arkansas or something, all decorated up for Christmas. Then ten years or so later aliens land—"

"Aliens?" Alamo chimed in, "Aliens from where?"

"From Uranus," Carnage responded, inevitably. We all laughed and Arthur got on with his proposition.

"Suppose these aliens—from Uranus—landed, and all they could find was these malls full up with crap to buy and all decorated up for Christmas. Then one day they decided to build a museum dedicated to Earth before the Great Disaster. This is what they would build. Having only the Christmas malls out in the boondocks to go on, Dollywood is what they would come up with."

I saw Jo-Jo peering around with his blue lips, and his red hands jammed into his pockets. He was considering Arthur's speech, nodding slowly, gravely, his mop of unruly hair cascading down his inclined forehead. He said, very slowly, very distinctly, "Mother Fucker." It was a kind of "amen."

Dolly herself was singing "Go Tell It on the Mountain" from a loudspeaker hidden in the crotch of a tree. All the people who had been poor and ignorant and miserable in real life were here transformed into Christmas gnomes, jolly and fragrant, offering the myriad comforts, manning the near-infinity of cash registers. All you needed was a credit card, and everyone had that. Dolly was the one who had made it out. Dolly was the goddess who had passed through fire and death, through paparazzi and face lifts, through Nashville and Hollywood, then turned back with her arms full of bounty, blessing and forgiving, transfiguring the past so that everyone who had come out of those dead coal mines and exhausted farms could imagine that they had traveled the same road and arrived at the same place as she. She had given them salvation that did not change what they were, but implied that what they were was plenty good enough, could its credos be sung in harmony sweet enough, could Jesus be thanked and welcomed by them often enough, could it all be powdered with enough glitter. Dolly was a Moses who marched the masses out of Egypt and back to Egypt again in a tight little loop going nowhere, but changing Egypt in the meanwhile into a Canaan hung with colored lights and peopled by figures out of books, so that you could think you had the whole while been sojourning to the Promised Land. Mee-Maw smashed the last hard autumn apples into mush to spread on your bread through the winter, but you could buy nine dollar Tahitian Island preserves that were supposed to be just like home because there was a picture of a crone in a sunbonnet stirring jelly on a wood-fire stove on the snow white label. Mee-Maw saved her pennies for milk for the baby, but you could idle in mile-long lines and buy a new coat for three dollars less at the Eddie Bauer outlet store. The Theme Park around us celebrated all that: thrift which was still thrift though it went forth in a jangle of unnecessary possessions, country values that were still country values even if you brought them out for Thanksgiving and Christmas only, piety that was still piety even though it was aimed at a sixteen year old Santa Christ leading the parade of toy soldiers into Toyland.

As if he had been listening to my thoughts, Jo-Jo muttered again, "Mother Fucker," leaning against the tree Dolly was singing in, trying through his cold skin and raw bones to understand.

We were glad for the rides and coasters. They had themes too, runaway coal cars and haunted mines, but you could ignore the themes and just ride. They were neutral, exciting, like the modern world, like my world. I thought about this. I wondered what if the aliens came and found only my dorm room left, and tried to construct a world out of that. Empty bottles would assume an inordinate centrality. If my hard drive survived, they might assume everybody was naked and looked like Pamela Anderson. I hoped we weren't in a wreck on 40 that night. I longed to get back to the room in time to change, or at least to enrich, the memory of our world before the volcanos cast finality over all.

Jo-Jo had no stomach for rides, and he stood with his hands jammed in his pockets and his neck lowered down into his shoulders, stamping around against the cold while we rode. I was glad for that, actually, glad to have something to look at—the way a dancer spots on a single place so she doesn't puke—as we spun and overturned. Jo-Jo as the center of my world was not what I'd anticipated, but there you are.

And I did vomit, copiously, carefully, under the pine trees that were probably planted there for that purpose, and the taste was taken away by the cotton candy that Jo-Jo had ready for me when we staggered off the big coasters. That was the confirmation I'd wanted, and it was comforting, despite everything. The trip was a success for me.

Alamo said I was the only one in the whole park throwing up. I didn't believe him, but even if it were true it made me special in some way I will be able to figure out before I ride my next ride.

Night is beautiful in Dollywood, all the trees become Christmas trees, all the buildings lined with blue and red fire, a parade made of long-eared elves and giant mice driving crazy cars winding through at the appointed hour. The evening hours of our visit found us dazed and exhausted, but we held on, wanting to drink that cup to the very dregs. We had long since stopped talking with our first excited energy, too, except for Alamo, who was ride-mad, and kept extolling the virtues of this or that brand of centrifugal peril. At the end we all stood with Jo-Jo on the pavement while Alamo got in one last turn on the coaster. I admired him. He was happy. He jogged in circles around us like a puppy, and though the park was closing, he kept gazing back wistfully at the wheels and parabolas glittering in the purple air. I think he had missed the philosophical discussion that so colored our perception of Dollywood. I think he was waiting in line for the Mystery Mine the second or third time. Power to him.

Slight rearrangement was necessary on the way home. I retained shotgun because of my knee, but Alamo was moved from the middle of the back seat to one of the windows. Alamo did not customarily use toiletries, and after a day like we'd had, it began to show, and it was important to have him to one side so the smell was as little pervasive as it could be. Alamo knew he smelled and initiated the change himself, so there were no hard feelings. He kept his window cracked the whole way, which was OK because we preferred the draft to Alamo's worn-a-little-too-long T-shirt. He was revved up about the rides, so he chattered on a little after we hit the road, admiring me because I rode and puked and yet rode again, but before the lights of Pigeon Forge faded, we had all subsided into a going-home-after-a-long-day stupor. Carnage, who had violent clothing but a clear conscience, was asleep almost immediately, scrunched up against Jo-Jo in a way that, for Jo-Jo, was a form of conversation.

The homeward road lay dark and bare, the world become rolling black hills against an almost black sky, stabbed here and there by the lights of houses or isolated strip malls. Deer stood on the roadside, wise deer who waited for us to pass before they darted out on their swift nocturnal ways. From the sounds of breathing I guessed everyone in back was asleep. Arthur slipped a disk in, and at first my innards tightened with disappointment. It was classical. He was driving, though, and it was his right to pick the music, and he had, after all, waited till everyone was asleep to indulge himself in this secret preference. He set the music low, and it amazed me to find myself poking the volume button a few times to hear it better.

"Bach," Arthur said. "Bach was a—"

"I know who Bach was. Why the hell did you pick—"

"Everybody's asleep. It's soothing."

Ba da da da da Ba da da da da—

It wasn't soothing me. I know I sounded gruff, but it was a long day, and the throw-up had burned my throat a little. I was listening. The music was long, ten, twenty times longer than a song on my iPod, but it was still one piece, an entity, rolling out, unfolding in the comfortably smelly dimness of the car. It was a song nobody was singing, of course, violins and . . . and lots of other stuff. God, I was ignorant. I didn't know what I was hearing. What the principle of it was. I could have asked Arthur, but the tone was set already, the tone of sleep and secret thoughts, and I was not going to break it for that. Arthur's hand reached for the eject button, and his voice said, "Do you want me to—?" But I said, "No. Leave it." I wanted it to sound like a concession, but it was really a request. I wanted to hear. I didn't understand what I was hearing, or why it affected me as it did. It was the opposite of Dollywood. I knew that, but if prof were in the car demanding that I be able to explain, I would have flunked in an instant.

"Does anybody ever sing?"

"Oh yes, of course, there are cantatas for every—"

I waved my hand to make him stop. It was meant as a criticism rather than an inquiry. Arthur could be very exhausting. He didn't pick up the cues.

The unaccustomed music moved me and I didn't know why. It was about something in a way most of my tunes were not. It was a lecture, only the lecturer didn't care if you were listening, and nobody took attendance. It was information. It was one side of a conversation, waiting for me to respond, which I would have had I known how. The strings said, Riley . . . Riley

. . .calling my name with that little upward lilt they had. I could hear them, but I didn't know how to answer. I wished there were a book somewhere where all this was written out. Maybe there was. I couldn't believe my own ignorance. I'd ask Arthur when the spell was off.

"Riley?"

Arthur's voice sounded resonant and portentous in the dark.

"Yeah?"

"I thought it was awful. Horrendous. Terrifying."

"What was? Dollywood?"

"Yeah. I'm sorry. I just don't get it."

"You don't?"

"You could help me."

A succession of white slashes passed under the car, lit by the lonely blaze of headlights. I didn't know what to say

"I figured you could take the news. The others. . . It would be like telling them there is no Santa Claus. Though, in fact, I've never been convinced about that one. You know my dad steal sneaks into the living room Christmas Eve after I've gone to bed and hangs up a stocking on the same old nail?"

"No, I didn't know that, Arthur."

"You pissed at me?"

"I've always admitted that you're way smarter than me. This is the first time you've used that intelligence to mock something I hold sacred."

I could feel Arthur deflating from across the seat.

"Oh, Christ I didn't mean that at all–"

"I know. Just let me sit here and think for a moment."

Arthur released a long sigh and glued his face back onto the winding Tennessee road before us.

I'd impressed myself with my passionate—if a little disingenuous—defense of Dollywood. I didn't want to say anything. Truth was, I found it terrifying too, but also that it was a kind of betrayal, a kind of uppityness to have said so. Dolly held her arms out to you, palms up, glittering with treats and souvenirs. If you hungered asked for something to eat she would rustle it up. Dolly told you that the way you always were was good enough. She said, "Come on over darlin'. I know what you wanted, and I suppose that's what you'll always want, and I got plenty of it."

Arthur's CD made no reference to anything like that. Johann Sebastian said, "Here is another world. Come hither. Run the other away. I don't care. Take it or leave it. Whatever you are, I still am as I have always been. People come the whole way to me and find the journey worth it. It is strange, arrogant, difficult and beautiful on the road I lead you. Other roads are familiar, comfortable, humble and pretty. I know where you are. I don't care. I have sung my song. You come or stay. I don't care. You decide. Mee-maw's Christmas tree lies that way. I lead another way. No promises. I'm saying nothing but what I say."

I was thinking so hard I didn't notice when my belly began to ache. Arthur heard me rustling in my seat.

"Your stomach still upset from the rides?"

He wanted to know if he had to pull over. I said, "A little. But I'm all right."

Five seconds later I said, as firmly as I could. "Pull over. Now."

I don't know what it was I was throwing up. Everything that went down had come up already, so I thought. But my body was finding ammunition somewhere, and when that ran out, there I was bent over at midnight in the wilderness, dry-heaving with a sound that, itself, made one sick. Ribbons of junk were hanging out of my mouth, the way it does, and Arthur was handing me Kleenex to take care of it. The headlights beamed into the distance, across a field of some low silage crop glittering with dew. The lights went a really long way and hit, so I thought, the pitched roof of a shed at the far end of the field.

When I reached back to take another Kleenex. I heard something that was not the sound of my own retching. In the dark close by, out of the range of the headlights and far enough away not to be lit by the open car door, something was moving. Though it had to be a cow or an old farm dog or something, I was seized with terror I couldn't explain. The sound was wrong. Whatever body had made it was not . . . was not familiar to me. My stomach wanted another go, but I held it off long enough to peer into the darkness. Perhaps something had been attracted to the sound of my sickness, the way predators are drawn to the sick and the weak. I held my breath. I could feel the acid run upwards on the inside of my throat, but if I were vomiting fire I would have held it off to get a clear view of what was moving toward me in the darkness. Bach was still playing inside. It was sinister now, metallic and precise, like the flight of an arrow. It didn't care about me. As I bent over to have another go, I saw it. Eyes appeared at the edge between dark and light, eyes kindled by the car, Four. Six. They were high off the ground, higher than a deer, higher than a man. Behind them were dark masses, big bodies, massive and built wrong for the normal things I knew, hesitating that final moment, deciding just then whether to lurk or to dash suddenly into the light.

"*Go! Go! Go!*" I was screaming, slamming the door behind me. I'd frightened Arthur so bad it took him a second to remember how to drive, and in that second something came out of the field which had been given back to the dark by the shutting of the car door. I felt something touch the handle. I was screaming and pushing against Arthur to get as far from the door as I could. The guys in back were wide awake now, looking around for the wreck we must have been in to cause all that furor.

"*Go! Go! Go!*"

Arthur spun the tires on the wet grass and finally made it to the road. He eased off a little until I screamed *Go!* I looked back through the open window. Alamo peered back through his window, too, looking up alternately at me for some clue as to what the fuck the matter was.

"What the—"

"There was something out there."

Someone in the back seat began to snicker. They were taking it as a joke. They thought I had started screaming the way you do in the dark just to scare the piss out of your buddies.

Carnage said, "That was a good one."

Arthur had made a couple of sharp turns on the winding road. He said, "It's the goddamn CD. That's the problem now. The goddamn Bach." He hit the eject button. There was midnight quiet, filled only by the sounds of innocent sleepers in the dark behind.

Carnage lived off campus, and was the first to be let off. Jo-Jo elbowed him a couple of time, until he gathered his tattered khakis around him and rolled out of the back seat. He stood for a moment, rubbing his eyes like a sleepy child. Someone in the house had kept the light on for him. We backtracked a little toward campus. Arthur found a parking spot near the dorms, and we piled out. Arthur stood with the back door open to air it out a little after Alamo disappeared into the night. He reached into his pocket and pulled out a roll of mints. I took a couple. My breath must have been awful.

"We didn't make bad time."

"No."

"What time is it, anyway?"

"Fuck the time. What was all that back there?'

"Art, I saw something. Out in the field when I was– I saw something."

Arthur was quiet for a while, and then he said, "You know, Dollywood wasn't a complete bust. There were things I liked."

"Yeah, what?"

Very slowly, as though it were a poem and he explicating it for class, he said, "That blue tree. The sycamore hung with lights, so at sunset, before it was really dark and you could tell they were lights, you thought it was really a blue tree. It had me. I was standing far away at first trying to figure out what kind it was. Trying to remember what country had trees like that, and what would a forest look like, and how could I get there. Blue. Weird winter blue. I liked that."

"Arthur, you are a piece of work."

"So you say. You feeling better?"

"Yeah."

I gathered my things up. Arthur helped me. I guess I was still a little sick. We were in separate dorms. I regretted this, because I didn't want to be alone in the dark the length of time it took me to get to mine.

"You want me to walk you home?

"Yeah."

I was relieved to have Arthur beside me. The night was sweet and, for a college campus, quiet. When we were almost at my door Arthur said, "I saw them too."

"The monsters? Out in the field?"

The look on his face was strange. He shrugged and said. "Monsters? That's not what I saw. I watched them in the starlight crossing the field, the whole time you were sick. The great, strange bodies. I thought maybe they had heard the Bach. I thought maybe they were coming for me. So I could see them, just this once. Their kind. They were so beautiful—"

His voice turned down at the end with such theatrical sadness I looked at him to see if he were joking. He wasn't. Arthur play-punched me in the jaw and then turned his back, heading toward his sleep with that little behind-the-back wave he had, which was sadder and more ambiguous at midnight than he probably understood. I wanted to call after him. I wanted to settle the matter of the creatures in the field. But I was afraid, standing there by myself, afraid even to call out lest the wrong thing hear. I punched in my code and opened the door.

The Gulf of Mexico

John Saad

Last winter, we walked
the fumbled light of live oaks,
where saw palmetto spurs

the understory by
fingerbreadths, then, unable
to hold, issues forth

the beach. We sat
before a rooted
sun, regathering

our pace and the words
we lost in the sands
of ground teeth. I found

a moment when love
overfills a gull's shadow
before we call it shade:

your arms clasped around
your knees, your body
like curled confessions—

and I forgave the Gulf
its familiar strangeness,
a dream of home with rooms

you never knew existed.
But it's too much for

me now, the horizon's

great flicker. The shoreline
gives rise in me
to draw back from myself—

from us—and hide in
the backwater pith,
the fluted boles of cypress,

a gull in the hem of dunegrass.

Karate in the Garage

John Saad

With the door rolled up and the bikes cleared out,
we splinter slats and pummel pumpkins with comet
punches and hammer heels. And when my anklet
rakes over Donnie's elbow, he sneers and shouts,
Your form is a goddamn dumpster fire! then darts
to his Mazda's mirror and lip balms his fu manchu.
Cross-legged, we cool down like vacuum tubes,
musing the plastic bonsai and the humming arc
of the water heater's flame. But our Zen was Cream
of Wheat until we ordered our gis and belts
with JEFF & DONNIE'S RECLAIMED KARATE in felt.
Because a dying art is a dilettante's dream,
we roundhouse the hanging tennis ball each night,
then take out the garbage, hoping for a streetfight.

The Sow-Taker

John Saad

Winter scores the politics
of meat, when hunters bring hogs

to Mr. Spiller so his neighbors
might eat. "That old man has seen

the world and never left
these woods," they like to say,

as if one old man carrying
a greasy come-along

and a burrstone name can all
alone keep the woods, the hamlet,

hell, the state! Deep in the pines,
his winch and chains hang slack

as chimes from a magnolia's
bottom limbs, just above

a hoisting gall. The tree's backside
drops dried-up crescent gourds

and the braided blackness
of coachwhip skin. Tonight,

he's due a sow or two,
so he lolls in a nook

of naked roots, through half-sleep
and hiccupping winds, the night's

mobile of stars and a lowing
Tenn-Tom barge. Yet enough

awake to thumb through his lists,
pruning those that have passed,

he notes what names are next
and who still owes him from last spring.

The Séance

Cathy Rose

"She's clairvoyant from birth," my mother said to her bridge party while I lay awake, kept up by the late-night tipsy laughter of ladies playing cards in our living room.

Moeder Eva lived at the end of our street in a modest clapboard house, and we lived in a brick one not unlike it. But while our house was filled with all that was ordinary and predictable about life in suburban Virginia, Moeder Eva's was infused with something mysterious and profound. When I was eight, my mother became a regular at this Dutch woman's prayer meetings, or so they were called when my mother spoke of them to the more conservative members of our community. These gatherings were actually séances, communications with spirits from the other side. On the first Saturday of every month, Moeder Eva gathered up a group of local ladies to pull the veil aside. Out on the enclosed sun porch, around a table built without the use of a single power tool by Eva's master craftsman husband, hands were held, eyes were shut tight, as Eva evoked the spirits.

"Oh, brotherhood of departed souls, guardians of the Akasha, we humbly request your presence."

I remember the ladies' stiff upright postures around the long table, their expectant faces freshly powered, the hum and whoosh of the air condition-ing unit, the goose bumps on all our sleeveless arms. The dogwood trees outback were in bloom. It must have been in spring.

"Our hearts are open, our intentions pure. Ladies, please join me—"

"Our hearts are open, our intentions pure—"

"Louder, ladies—our hearts are open—"

My mother was the youngest of the women who attended Moeder Eva's meetings. The others all had children old enough to have their own places to go on a Saturday afternoon. So Moeder Eva delighted in me and me alone. While the women convened over tea and cakes, she would let me clop around in the giant wooden shoes she kept by the front door, and play with the little Dutchman with the bobbing head on her mantelpiece. And in my teacup she would always drop a round Droste chocolate. "A sweets for the sweet," she would say spraying the top of my head with tiny bits of saliva.

During the séance, I did not sit up at the table, but played on the floor below, with the dolls I brought from home, a beehive doo Barbie, a crew cut

Ken, a Midge, two Skippers, and the muscular, double-jointed GI Joe. The ladies' legs beneath the séance table were my post and pillar. But I also saw all that they probably did not want me to, the slant of their worn heels, the creeping runs in their nylons. My mother's ankles were noticeably delicate, her shoes simple, but made in faraway countries like France and Italy. These were places my mother wanted to go, though I'm not sure she knew just why.

"We request a visit from the deceased, Anneke Van Schoonhoven, sister of my moeder, who died of poor conditions and ill health in the town of Rotterdam, in the year 1952. Ladies, join me. We request a visit from Anneke Van Schoonhoven—"

"From Anneke Van SH-KOO—on-hoven—"

I am not certain how Moeder Eva and her husband made it from their small island town off the mainland of the Netherlands to our little street in the heart of Tidewater, Virginia. If Moeder Eva spoke of Nazi invasions, of the destruction of her country and its people during the War, it most likely escaped my mother altogether. There was never any sense of history in our family, of our own or anyone else's, even though history runs like floodwater through this region of the South.

"Who are the great beings from Amer-IK-a you would like to consult?" Moeder Eva would sometimes ask after she had exhausted her own reper- toire of spirits from the old country. "George Washington, Thomas Jeffer- son, Sir Walter Raleigh," the ladies would call out, like eager-to-please school children.

"Amelia Earhart," my mother, who had never stepped foot on a plane much less crossed an ocean, once tentatively requested.

"Well, what do you want to ask her, dear?"

"I don't know, I hadn't thought of what—"my mother said, her heel lifting cautiously out of her pump. And, I think she finally asked a question for my father—would his office indeed move across town into the site of the Old First National Bank. And whatever answer the spirits gave, I'm sure it was never shared at home. My father did not want to know the details of our shenanigans, as he called them. He tried to ignore my mother's dreaminess, tried to deny it away. And yet, you couldn't help but see her still frame before the living room window as the evening approached, couldn't help but hear the wistful sighs over a slow boiling pot on the stove.

Most of the questions posed to Moeder Eva during the séances were ones I did not understand or that did not concern me—would a person's health improve, was a financial investment wise or foolish, would there be peace on earth or calm in the troubled lives of one of the ladies in the group. "Oh, selfless beings, guardians of the Akasha . . . you are such a gift!" I would say to my dolls sometimes, imitating, but never mocking Moeder Eva.

If it had not been for the sudden shifting of legs under the table, the excited, stolen glances down onto the floor where I was playing, I might not have heard Moeder Eva's spirits at all, when one day, they spoke of me.

"Ladies, eyes closed! I have entered the Hall of Records!" Moeder Eva scolded rapping the table with the end of a teaspoon and swaying from side to side. I was used to Moeder Eva's séance voices, to the sexless personalities that slid one into another in a kind of run-on singsong chant. Ordinarily, I just tuned them out. But the sudden commotion under the table, and Eva's rapping combined in an instant to make me jump half out of my skin. I reached for my doll. "Hear ye, hear ye!" Ken called out to Barbie and the others who gathered round, "I have entered the Hall——of——Records!"

I am not sure how my Hall of Records compared to Moeder Eva's from behind the veil. Mine, I know, looked a lot like the massive fluorescent-lit college library where my father had taken me when he wanted to research a new tax law. Moeder Eva's Hall was probably much grander, like the British Museum or the Smithsonian.

"The little girl chi——ld among you . . . has a special des——tiny. She is an old so——oul and will gro——woo up to serve——"

I did not know what a destiny was, but I could tell by the way Moeder Eva spoke the word that it was an important thing, and a special thing that I had. My mother had not spoken up once since the day of Amelia Earhart, and so I was startled now to hear her.

"Where–where might she travel?" my mother said, winding her foot around her ankle. I thought then of all the odd shaped vases and polished figurines from exotic places like Egypt, South America, and India that my mother had placed on the shelves above our television set and on the table beside my father's easy chair. My father made fun of these objects and knocked them onto the floor "accidentally on purpose," according to my mother, as he adjusted the rabbit ears on our console TV.

"She will go . . . she will go——to the Nay———derlands," Moeder Eva said smiling and swaying more now, as if to a tune. "Oh yes, the Nay———derlands."

I knew, of course that this was Moeder Eva's beloved homeland. "I will go," I said to myself, looking over at the bobble head Dutchman with new interest, "to the Nay——derlands." But whatever rush of excitement I felt in that moment was quickly replaced by sadness. While I would travel to the Netherlands, it seemed when I was grown, I knew my mother most likely never would, nor would she travel to any of the other exotic places she dreamed of. My father had told her many times, he wasn't made of money, and this would always be true, I thought.

"And to the thick jungles of Af——rica, where she will develop a deeeeeep relation——ship with the animal king——dom, and she will travel to Indi—Indi——let me consult the Hall . . . India—no,——In——dohhhhh——neeez—YAH!" Moeder's Eva head fell forward, then snapped back up. "But Re——re—gar—ding love—the love between man—and—wooooo–man for this child," Moeder Eva continued. "I am checking the Akashic records . . ."

My face grew hot when Eva mentioned love. I did not speak of my longings to anyone back then. And I was afraid of what the spirits knew of Barbie and GI Joe, of their tender words to each other, and of a kiss behind the leg of the séance table.

"Love will be diff——diff——difficult, however," Moeder Eva continued. "She will gain much reck———COG——nition for her good works, but there will not be a deeep com——MOON—ee—ON with, she will take no huz—no huz——no HUZ—band in this lifetime."

I do not remember the séance after that, though I believe it continued on for quite some time. But I recall how strange it was afterwards to be in Moeder Eva's living room with the ladies laughing and talking about shopping bargains and recipes while my mind reeled with what the spirits had said about me, about my lifetime. And I think it was a lifetime my mother was quite proud of because across the room, she called me to her, drew me up close and said, "I love you, sweetheart, you are my very special girl."

And my eyes filled with tears then, and I wanted to stay in my mother's arms a long while, and to whisper in her ear so that no one, not even Moeder Eva's spirits could hear, that I was frightened of Africa, and did not want a DES-tiny, or to go to that Indo—Indo—neez—YAH, where there would be no one, not ever, to cherish me.

Inner Bean

Kevin Rabas

We play
Dave Matthews' "Crash,"
  & are not asked back.

The coffee shop's
  more Christian
than we thought.

T's voice ain't great,
  but he sings
with his heart
  in his throat,
his blonde guitar
  hot in light,
his fingers fast,
  young Turk,
kid with six coins
  and lint
in his pocket;
  my drumsticks
in shreds, my brushes bent,
  we come and go,
like sons that limp home
  and don't look back.

High Dive
Jason R. Kesler

How did I get here? the boy asked himself.

A nervous laugh broke from his nostrils.

One minute he had been down in the shallow end, looking up at the monstrosity that towered over the pool, like the skeletal remains of some prehistoric dinosaur he had learned about in school—the brontosaurus. He'd been watching the older boys climb the brontosaurus's neck one vertebra at a time, making their way to the skull where they would hold on to the dinosaur's orbital bones on each side of the head before stepping onto the jaw that jutted out over the chlorinated lagoon, and—

Then Tommy North yelled, "You have been babbutized!"

Jimmy was smacked in the forehead. Everything went wobbly after that, and he'd found himself up there looking down at the pool, several epochs away.

No one was looking back. No one had noticed.

For a moment, the boy wondered if he wasn't imagining himself on that high dive. He lifted his arms out in front of him and looked at his hands, palms up, palms down. *This is my body.* The wind whipped at his hair. His oversized red swimsuit flapped against his calves. *This is my body broken on the concrete.*

He could see it—his body—from atop the high dive all busted up down below, his arms and legs splayed in uncomfortable angles. The sight made him grip the metallic railing again.

You're more than a body. That's what Mr. Biffen, his Sunday school teacher, had said. *You're a boy. You're a son. You've been given a name. You've been given a soul.*

But didn't he have these things because he had a body? Before he'd been born, had he been a boy, a son? Did he have a name before he was born, or a soul? He didn't know. So if you didn't have a body anymore, would you still have these other things, too?

Contemplating the way forward, the boy noticed that the railing he was holding for reassurance only went halfway out to the end of the diving board. In order to make it to the water, he'd have to travel the length of the board, and to do *that* without the railing, he would have to rely on his balance. As far as he knew, his balance was good. He'd walked the beam at the Fun Tyme Gym where his little sister went for gymnastics and had not fallen off. Even so, the practice beam was just a few inches off the ground and there was padding underneath.

But not up here. His only options were the water or the concrete. And he wasn't inches off the ground, either. He was feet and feet and feet. A gust of wind tugged at his swimsuit again. He held on tighter to the railing on his right side. His arms were too short to hold onto both rails at the same time.

He could run for it. By the time he fell, he'd be near the end of the high dive, right? The water would be there to break—his neck.

The boy swallowed hard.

That was something else he hadn't thought of. How do you fall from such a great height? What if he belly-flopped? Would his abdomen rip open and his guts spill out into the pool? How would he ever recover them? What if he got turned around in the air and landed upside down on his head? Could his brain break?

It was while he was counting the gruesome injuries he might incur from this stupid stunt that people on the ground began to see him up there. He had become quite the spectacle. The kids in his swim class, having changed back into their street clothes, were gradually trickling out of the bathrooms. Somebody's mother asked Somebody, "Who's that up there?" It was hard to tell. The sun, sliding down the western sky, was obscuring the boy's features. So one kid nudged another kid and another and pointed up to the top of the high dive until finally one of them just said it: "That's Jimmy."

Jimmy didn't notice that he'd been spotted and identified until the chanting began. It drifted to his position on the high dive sounding like a faintly whispered suggestion—the hint of an idea planted in his subconscious while he was sleeping—then it became more insistent: "jump, jimmy, jump, jimmy, jump, JUMP, JIMMY, JUMP, JIMMY, JUMP."

He looked down to see the gathering crowd looking up at him. There was that Tommy North kid again. His dad was a city councilman. His family lived in one of the nicest houses in the neighborhood with a finished basement that had a game room with a pool table. Jimmy saw Eric Williamson, who could ollie a skateboard as high as . . . well, higher than anybody. Trevor Rowe was there, too. He was one of the best Cub Scouts in his troop. He had twice as many merit badges as anyone else. And Mark Green, the friendliest guy Jimmy knew. He could talk (and talk and talk), especially about his comic book collection: *Boris the Bear* and *The Teenage Mutant Ninja Turtles*.

What if it was one of them who was up there looking down at *him*? What would Eric or Trevor or Mark or any of them think of him? What was Jimmy? Absolutely nothing came to mind. He was a nobody—just a shy kid who hadn't done anything of any importance.

But that was about to change. Jimmy closed his eyes and took a deep breath.

◆

Ron Driver was just a voice at first: "If the dummy don't wanna dive, I'll th'ow him off." Then he became a tiny metallic ping made by his meaty hands slapping against the diving board's railings. And then Ron became a tremor as his heavy feet hit each rung of the ladder all the way up to the top of the board. This seismic prescience transferred to Jimmy's legs and from there to his other extremities.

So he was already shaking when Ron's rather large head came level with the diving board. "Hey, kid," he said in a commanding baritone that meant business.

Jimmy's nostrils flared like a spooked horse's, and he gripped the railing tighter.

"Jesus Christ, don't go splattering yourself all over the place."

Being reminded of the potential his body had of becoming abstract art on the concrete canvas below didn't help calm Jimmy's quivering legs.

Neither did Ron's demeanor. He was a brutish boy—a man-child, really. Ron was one of those overgrown ogres who had hit puberty—busted right through it—a year or two early. At the age of twelve, he already had hair on his upper lip, and not just a feathery dusting of it either. It was dark, particularly at the corners of his mouth, and it made him look dangerous, villainous.

"So, you gonna jump or what?" Ron said the question without asking it.

Jimmy swallowed before answering. "I don't know."

"Well, you're holding up the show."

"Sorry." Jimmy's teeth were chattering too much to say more.

Ron snorted at Jimmy's attempted apology. There was a flash of red fire burning in Ron's eyes. It was there and it was gone. Must have been some trick of light, Jimmy thought.

Ron stretched his neck from side to side trying to work out a strategy. A gutsy move would be to just charge the kid, bully him off the board. If they were on the playground at school, that's what Ron would have done, but his formidable size up in the air wasn't quite the advantage that it was down on the ground. A little finesse would be required, but *little* and *finesse* were concepts not associated with Ron Driver. As Ron hesitated, Jimmy could sense that somehow he had the upper hand up here.

All Ron had was talk. "Whatever you do," he finally said, a gust of wind curling a lock of his hair on the top of his head, "it's gonna be the talk of the town—from here to Hoschton Park. Everybody's gonna want to know what happened. You can bet I ain't gonna keep my mouth shut. So what do you wanna be: the youngest boy ever to jump from the Jackson Rec high dive or the biggest baby in all of Commerce, Georgia?"

Ron climbed up another step on the ladder and was now eye to eye with Jimmy.

"Heck, I'd let you sit beside me on the bus if you wanted, and I ain't let nobody do that. All you have to do is fall, really. Nothing to it. God and gravity will take care of the rest."

Jimmy eyed Ron eyeing him.

"I-I bet if you asked Him nicely, He'd send down some sweet angel down to carry you into the water."

Jimmy had his doubts about that. And anyway—"You're not supposed to talk about Him like that."

"Who says?" Ron heckled.

"The Bible," Jimmy said.

"The Bible don't say," Ron countered, "unless you read it aloud, and only dummies have to do that. Are you a dummy?" Jimmy didn't answer. "And anyway it don't look like you got one up here so . . ."

But Jimmy wasn't listening. He was thinking of his Bible—the one he'd been given to commemorate his christening, the one he was afraid to open by himself for fear God might pop out of it—was safe and sound on the bookshelf in his bedroom at home. He wished he could zap himself back there right now before swim practice had ever happened. Jimmy wondered if he prayed for that—

"So what are you gonna do? Stay up here foreverandever?" Ron tried to make the question sound like a challenge.

No. Jimmy knew that was the right answer, but he didn't say it. He was fixated on *foreverandever*. It seemed such a funny thing to say. A sing-song sort

Illustration by Nolen Otts

of fairytale incantation. Was there any magic to it, and if so was it a blessing or a curse? Coming out of Ron's mouth, it sounded like nonsense.

A drop of sweat slid down his shoulder blade. Jimmy's knees shimmied a little. He felt the subtle strain of his muscles operating just underneath his abdomen. Jimmy had to pee. He would have to make a decision soon. The ticking of the internal clock in his mind got louder, each tick a second, each second a chance, each chance a risk . . . Now that he was up there, the way he got down was important. Ron was right about that. Jimmy was gonna be the talk of the town after this. There was no going back to being a nobody. He knew what he wanted to do—who he wanted to be. The spirit was willing . . . but the flesh was weak. His body, this stupid thing that had its own feelings, its own needs was insensate to reason. It wouldn't let him. There was no convincing it to do what instinctively it knew it did not want to do.

Jimmy had gone into the shell of the self. No amount of berating or coaxing from Ron was going to get him to budge. He was out of his depth up there on that high dive so he sent out a parting shot—"You're one tough nut, kid!"— in Jimmy's direction before going back down the ladder.

◆

Then his mother wandered out of the snack shack with one hand over her eyes to shade them from the sun, the other hand dragging, Joanna, Jimmy's younger sister—both *her* hands wrapped around the wax paper wrapping of the pickle she was eating—in tow. It took the mother a moment, but she finally saw it: her own boy standing up there on the diving board. She started then thought to wave but then thought better of it. Jimmy's mother continued moving in the direction of the deep end, until she found one of the lifeguards set apart from the rest of the kids now crowded at the bottom of the ladder by the whistle lodged between her lips, not her size.

Little Jeannie Luster listened to what Jimmy's mom had to say, then she blew her whistle and gave instruction: "Step away from the high dive."

The boys in the group didn't like being shooed away by any girl—particularly Little Jeannie who was barely taller than they were—but most of them were happy to have their hands washed of any future responsibility. They made way for her to walk to the ladder.

Little Jeannie cupped her hands around her mouth and called to Jimmy, "Your mother and sister are here, and they want to see you."

From this great height, his mother didn't look like his mother. She was as small as the lifeguard, as small as the rest of the crowd. They were like one big unhappy family down there, all except Joanna, who looked like Joanna. Uncomfortable with crowds, she had her head down and was chipping away at that pickle one chomp at a time. Jimmy imagined he could hear the crunch and smell the stink of Joanna's pickle-breath. He didn't like pickles, but even so, he had to smile. He liked his sister alright . . . when he wasn't having to "entertain" her. That's what Jimmy's mother called it—entertainment—when Joanna begged and begged to play with his Matchbox cars, when he just wanted to play by himself. Neither the two of them—mother, sister —understood that he wasn't playing. It was serious business. Jimmy had designed a race track in the family's seldom-used living room that ran from the hardwood floors of the hallway, under the legs of the piano bench, around the coffee table and up the sofa—the arm, the back, the other arm—and down to the carpet again, and again and again. He kept a log of all the races to rank each car individually so at the end of the season, there'd be a winner. But Jimmy had to suspend a whole afternoon's schedule because of Joanna. She wouldn't listen to the rules, and her eyes would threaten him with tears if he tried to object. Jimmy didn't want Joanna as a sister then.

But now she seemed to be the only one uninterested in what was going on, the crown of her head a radiant sunflower in a field of sunburned faces that looked up at him. Jimmy wiped his sweaty palms on the legs of his red swimsuit. Except for his sister, he wished he could tell them all to go away, particularly his mother. She couldn't help him now—she could only make things worse.

◆

But it wasn't her fault when worse—in the form of Vince McKeel, the Assistant Director of the Jackson County Park and Recreations Department—did make his appearance. It was Little Jeannie Luster's whistle that must have called him out of his office in the nearby administration building. Jimmy squinted as the fat, balding man wearing a tight, blue polo shirt and bulging khaki pants waddled over to the base of the high dive. Jeannie met him at the outer edge of the crowd and lowered her head as if to surrender the whistle around her neck because now that he was on the scene, there would be no more amateurish attempts at getting the boy to come down.

Jimmy's mother (and sister) joined the two in consultation. Mr. McKeel did most of the talking, his massive head bobbing up and down, the little hair he had clinging to his scalp like a wilted laurel wreath. Whatever he was saying, Jimmy's mother didn't like it. She shook *her* head and pointed off in the distance towards town. But McKeel wasn't taking orders; he was giving them. The assistant director broke the huddle and took off his thick glasses that had worked their way down to the point of his nose. He produced a handkerchief from his back pocket and swabbed his sweat-soiled face.

Jimmy looked to the horizon. The sun was hovering just above the trees that hemmed in the Mackie Jackson baseball field at the western edge of the rec department. This was where the big kids played ball before Hoschton Park opened with its nice metallic bleachers and state-of-the-art scoreboards. Now the Mackie Jackson was just a fenced in lot, the outfield grass the color of an old photograph, the infield dirt nothing but dry dust.

When he looked back down, Mr. McKeel had his glasses on again. The man cocked his head at an angle and called up the high dive's ladder, "Get down offa there buddy . . . please, now. You've got your mother here all worried about you." He looked at her and nodded, as if giving a cue to make some dramatic, emotional show.

But Jimmy's mother wasn't one for public displays. She brought the hand that wasn't holding onto her daughter up to her brow as if to salute her son then let it drop to her side again.

McKeel grimaced at the effort. He looked back up the ladder to see if her gesture had had any effect on the boy. It didn't look like it. "Did you hear me?"

Of course Jimmy could hear him. The man had the belly of a walrus and the bellow to match. Had Mr. McKeel asked a more pertinent question or offered some useful advice, Jimmy would have responded. He knew he had to get *offa* there, and he knew that his mother was worried. Those facts didn't change his inability to get his legs to move in either forward or backward direction. It was as if his feet were nailed to the board.

"Did you hear me?" McKeel repeated himself, but this time with a more forceful blast he usually reserved for swim team practice. "You don't want me coming up there," he added.

Jimmy could see that might be a problem. The man's weight could topple the high dive, killing both of them. The diving tower wasn't exactly new anymore. Metallic blue paint had flecking off its base, and some rust had collected around its bolted joints.

"You can't," Jimmy said, matter-of-fact.

McKeel must have felt that he was being teased. "Whaddaya mean I can't?" The man put a loafer on the bottom step of the ladder as if that alone would prove the boy wrong, but that was as far as he would go.

Jimmy's mother walked up behind him. She had a Snickers bar in her hand. The snack shack stored them in the refrigerator and sold them cold for a dollar. Jimmy's mother would bribe him with them, promising one at the end of each swimming lesson. She must have bought it along with Joanna's pickle and put the Snickers in her purse for safe-keeping. Jimmy the son loved his mother for her thoughtfulness, but he could not just think of himself as *that* Jimmy. There were other Jimmys to consider: Jimmy the coward, Jimmy the hero. But the situation offered more possibilities than this oppositional binary. There was a third option—Jimmy the trouble-maker—and even a fourth—Jimmy the problem child.

McKeel turned to face the mother. He grabbed the candy bar out of her hand and held it aloft, saying, "Take it. It's yours if you'll just come down."

Jimmy the boy was tempted by candy bar. He could feel it in his hands already—oddly cool to the touch at first but becoming lukewarm the longer he held it. The change in temperature changing the taste of the chocolate, the caramel—every bite of it a different experience.

Hungry for a quick resolution that would renew his authority, the assistant director chomped on the inside of his cheek, working a red rash into his jowls.

Jimmy saw it, and he looked away.

◆

A low, mournful wail reached his ears from a distance. For a moment, he thought someone was crying—that *he* was crying—but as the noise grew louder, Jimmy realized it was coming from down there. He scanned the crowd for a moment, thinking it might be his mother, but she was now crouching down, helping Joanna with a napkin. The other parents were talking to themselves, and their kids—bored with the will-he-or-won't-he dilemma—had begun to crowd at the fence, looking for what was coming next.

Jimmy saw it first—past the pool area and beyond the rec department parking lot. A vehicle with flashing colored lights was barreling up the street. The cops. Were they coming . . . for *him*? Jimmy was in real trouble now. He was gonna be arrested or worse and for what? Because he couldn't jump off a high dive? Was it a crime for a nine-year-old kid to be on a twelve-foot high dive? Was there some arithmetical rule—an appropriate ratio of age to height that the diving instructor had forgotten to mention? Were you only allowed on a diving board as tall as your age?

But Jimmy didn't think he was that lucky. If *only* the cops were coming for him. They could arrest him. Throw him in the slammer for a while. Maybe he'd be sent to juvenile detention where he'd never be heard from or seen again . . . or at least until the summer was over and somebody else had stumbled into something stupid.

But no one was coming to his rescue. He could see the left blinker lighting up on the squad car as it came to an intersection. He was all alone up there and out of reach. It was up to Jimmy to get himself down. But he didn't have to do it for God or the other kids or Ron or his mom or Mr. McKeel or anybody. He just had to do it. He closed his eyes one more time and said a private good-bye to the boy he used to be—the nobody he could no longer be.

So when the boys at the fence turned back around, they saw that the high dive didn't have nobody on it nomore. The boy they knew was gone . . .

Lunchroom Etiquette
Monika McGreal Viola

Again, these teachers are talking,
Idle chatter in the teacher's lounge.
Their mindless curiosities peck at my ears,
Their dizzy gossip sizzles my mind.

They're gabbing in the teacher's lounge, again
About "those progressives" and "women's rights",
Their gossip dizzies and sizzles my mind,
As I do an indignant burn.

"Those progressives" and "women's rights" make them
Mash their terrible teeth and roar their terrible roars.
Indignation flares then burns,
But they don't bother to lower their voices.

They mash their words and the roar is terrible,
One group of women mocking another.
They don't lower their voices — no bother,
Liberals aren't allowed inside the door.

Mockingly — Women's groups? Equal rights?
"Progressives," one spits out the word.
They speak with me outside the door (no liberals allowed),
To engage or not to engage, that is the question.

Pro-gress-ives — the word splits…
Idealism as a dirty word?
It's a question of disengaging.
And then, "I hate those Coexist bumper stickers."

Idealist is a dirty word
In these parts of town and when I hear
"I hate those Coexist bumper stickers,"
I decide to turn the corner.

In that part of town, I heard
Idle chatter in the teacher's lounge.
I've decided to turn a corner since
I heard those teachers talking.

Contributors

Marley Simmons Abril lives in Bellingham, Washington, where she is currently pursuing her MFA. Her work has appeared in *Jeopardy Magazine* and *Femeninete*, and she was awarded a flash memoir prize by *Cascadia Weekly*. She writes mainly short fiction, but also some flash fiction and prose poetry, and she teaches composition at WWU.

Colton Adrian is twenty-two. He plays with dirt at work and writes when he's not doing that. He escaped via C-section and was birthed in Williamsburg, Virginia. His most recent work has appeared in *Zone Other Magazine* and *The Buffalo Almanack*.

Regan Green is a rising sophomore at Samford University, originally from Columbia "Muletown," Tennessee. She is a science journalist for Samford's planetarium and has an internship with South Central Tennessee Tourism Association and recently published an article for a small magazine in her hometown called *Validity*.

David Brendan Hopes teaches at the University of NC, Asheville, where he is active in the local theater and arts scenes.

Scott Howdeshell lives and works in Central Alabama, making drinks and mopping floors. He loves his mother and his cat and music and Cormac Mc-Carthy.

Dan Jacoby is a graduate of St. Louis University, Chicago State University, and Governors State University. He lives both in Beecher and Hagaman, Illinois. He has published poetry in *Anchor and Plume* (Kindred), *Arkansas Review, Belle Rev Review, Bombay Gin, Canary, Cowboy Poetry Press-Unbridled 2015* (Western Writers Spur Award), *Chicago Literati, Indiana Voice Journal, Deep South Magazine, Lines and Stars, Wilderness House Literary Review, The Opiate*, and *Red Fez* to name a few. He is a former principal, teacher, coach, and former counterintelligence agent. He is a member of the American Academy of Poets. Nominated for a Pushcart Prize in 2015. He is currently looking for a publisher for a collection of poetry.

Ashley M. Jones earned an MFA in Poetry from Florida International University, where she was a John S. and James L. Knight Foundation Fellow. Her work has been published in various journals nationwide, and she was a 2015 Rona Jaffe Foundation Writer's Award Recipient. Her debut collection, *Magic City Gospel* is forthcoming from Hub City Press in 2017. She lives in Birmingham, Alabama, where she teaches creative writing at the Alabama School of Fine Arts.

Robert Lee Kendrick lives in Clemson, South Carolina. He has previously published, or has work forthcoming, in *Louisiana Literature*, *South Carolina Review*, *The James Dickey Review*, *Kestrel*, and *Main Street Rag*. His chapbook, *Winter Skin*, is forthcoming from Main Street Rag Publishing in June 2016.

Jason R. Kesler is currently pursuing an MFA in creative writing from the Sewanee School of Letters at the University of the South. He has never been on a high dive (as far as he can remember—perhaps he's blocked it out) and doesn't enjoy swimming all that much. Nevertheless, he is the proud uncle of a niece who recently dove off a diving board for the first time.

Len Kuntz is a writer from Washington State, an editor at the online magazine *Literary Orphans*, and the author of *I'm Not Supposed To Be Here and Neither are You* out now from Unknown Press. You can also find him at lenkuntz. blogspot.com.

Dan Leach's short fiction has been published in various literary journals and magazines, including *The Greensboro Review*, *Deep South Magazine*, and *The New Madrid Review*. A native of South Carolina, he graduated from Clemson University in 2008, and taught high-school in Charleston until 2014 when he relocated to Nebraska. *Floods and Fires*, his debut short-story collection, will be published by University of North Georgia Press in 2016.

Tim Nalley is a recent graduate in creative writing at The University of Alabama in Birmingham. His work has appeared in *Aura* and *Wingspan*. He lives in Odenville, Alabama with his family.

Heidi Espenscheid Nibbelink lives in Athens, Georgia. She grew up in Wisconsin and Wyoming, where she held various jobs such as sandwich artist, ice-cream scooper, oboist for hire, educational program assistant, and weekend music host at Wyoming Public Radio. She currently works as a counselor at an urban public high school. Her short fiction can be found online at *Drunk Monkeys*, *Shark Reef*, *1:1000*, *New Pop Lit*, and the *Nude Bruce Review*. She is an MFA student at the Sewanee School of Letters. You can follow her on Twitter @AnnoyedOboist or on her website: heidinibbelink.com.

Robert Okaji lives in Texas and is the author of *If Your Matter Could Reform* (Dink Press, 2015) and *The Circumference of Other*, which is included in *Ides: A Collection of Poetry Chapbooks* (Silver Birch Press, 2015). Publication credits include *Panoplyzine*, *Hermeneutic Chaos*, *MockingHeart Review*, and *Eclectica*, among others.

A native of western North Carolina, **Ellen Perry's** academic interests include 17th- and 18th-century British life and literature, Restoration drama, and Southern/ Appalachian culture. Her story "Milk, Bread, Soft Drinks" was awarded First Place in Fiction by the *Bacopa Literary Review*. Ellen enjoys reading, traveling, dancing, working on her collection of short stories, and playing with her stylish cat, Ms. Coco Chanel.

Kevin Rabas leads the poetry track at Emporia State University. He has seven books, including *Lisa's Flying Electric Piano*, a Kansas Notable Book and Nelson Poetry Book Award winner.

Cathy Rose's fiction has appeared in *Deep South Magazine*, *Fifth Wednesday Journal*, *Rosebud*, *Fourteen Hills*, *Santa Clara Review*, and elsewhere. She was recently awarded the Mary Elizabeth Nelson Fellowship at Rivendell Writers' Colony in Sewanee, TN. Raised in Williamsburg, VA, she now resides in San Francisco, CA where she is a psychologist in private practice.

Philip St. Clair is the author of six collections (books and chapbooks) of poetry. His work has appeared in *Beloit Poetry Journal*, *Black Warrior Review*, *Gettysburg Review*, *Harper's*, *Ploughshares*, *Prairie Schooner*, *Rattle*, *Shenandoah*, and elsewhere. Awards include the Bullis Prize from *Poetry Northwest* and grants from the National Endowment for the Arts and the Kentucky Arts Council. He has taught at Kent State University, Bowling Green State University, Southern Illinois University, and at present he is Professor Emeritus At Ashland Community and Technical College. He lives with his wife Christina in Ashland, Kentucky.

John Saad lives and works in Birmingham, Alabama, with his wife and their two dogs. His poetry has appeared recently in *Kudzu House Quarterly* and is forthcoming in *ISLE*. He writes poetry.

Claudia Serea is a Romanian-born poet who immigrated to the U.S. in 1995. Her poems and translations have appeared in *Field, New Letters, 5 a.m., Meridian, Word Riot, Apple Valley Review,* among others. Serea is the author of *Angels & Beasts* (Phoenicia Publishing, Canada, 2012), *A Dirt Road Hangs From the Sky* (8th House Publishing, Canada, 2013), *To Part Is to Die a Little* (Cervena Barva Press, 2015), and *Nothing Important Happened Today* (Broadstone Books, 2016). Serea co-hosts The Williams Readings poetry series in Rutherford, NJ. She is a founding editor of *National Translation Month*. More at cserea.tumblr.com.

A Pushcart Prize nominee, **Diane Thomas-Plunk** was also recognized by NPR when her entry was selected as a "favorite" in their *Three-Minute Fiction* contest. Thomas-Plunk's short stories and poetry have appeared in Belle Reve Literary Journal. Stories have also appeared in *The Dead Mule School of Southern Literature* and *China Grove Magazine. Deep South Magazine* has published multiple of her stories. Born and raised in Memphis, TN, Thomas-Plunk currently resides in north Mississippi.

Wendy Thornton is a freelance writer and editor who has been published in *Riverteeth, Epiphany, MacGuffin* and many other literary journals and books. Her memoir, *Dear Oprah Or How I Beat Cancer and Learned to Love Daytime TV,* was published in July 2013. She has won many awards for her work including most recently, second prize in New York's Literal Latte essay contest. She was nominated for a Pushcart Prize, and has been Editor's Pick on Salon.com multiple times. Her work is published in England, Scotland, Australia and India.

David Tuvell studied at University of Florida and has a BA in English from Kennesaw State University. His work has appeared or is forthcoming in *New Orleans Review*, *Minetta Review*, KSU's *Share*, and *Eyedrum Periodically*.

Monika McGreal Viola holds a B.A. from Brown University, and master's degrees in Fiction Writing from Johns Hopkins University and Anglo-Irish Writing from Trinity College, Dublin. Her work has appeared in *Hermeneutic Chaos*, *AZURE*, *PennUnion*, *Common Ties*, *Icarus Magazine*, and *Thirteen Ways Magazine*. Her poetry also has been twice shortlisted for the Fish Anthology Poetry Prize. Find her at www.monikamcgrealviola.com.

Richard Weaver's work has been published in *Conjunctions*, *Loch Raven Review*, *North American Review*, *Crazy Horse*, *BWR*, *2River View*, *Pembroke*, *New England Review*, and the ubiquitous Elsewhere.